The Big Chill

The Big Chill

Lawrence Kasdan and Barbara Benedek

St. Martin's Press

New York

Library of Congress Cataloging in Publication Data

Kasdan, Lawrence.
The big chill (1983).

(St. Martin's original screenplay series)
I. Benedek, Barbara.   II. Big chill (Motion picture)
III. Title.   IV. Series.
PN1997.B426   1987   791.43′72   86-27898
ISBN 0-312-00009-X (pbk.)

First Edition

10   9   8   7   6   5   4   3   2   1

The Big Chill

The screen is black.   -1-

The soft sounds of WATER LAPPING, small SPLASHES. Now comes
the VOICE OF A THREE YEAR-OLD BOY -- talking, laughing, and,
then, short bits of singing. A MAN'S VOICE chuckles in
response, coaxes gently for more.

FADE IN:

1   INT. BATHROOM, HAROLD AND SARAH'S HOUSE (RICHMOND, VIRGINIA)   1
                                                          -NIGHT

The little BOY is being given a bath. He plays with tub toys
and continues to sing as his father, HAROLD, soaps his silky
skin. This child, oddly enough, seems to know the words to
a Sixties rock song, "Joy to the World", by the group Three
Dog Night. He needs only intermittent coaching from his father.
They are both very happy.

In an adjacent bedroom, the telephone begins to ring. After a
few rings, SARAH picks it up. Harold glances in at his wife,
who he can see from his spot next to the tub. She is, like
her husband, in her early 30's. Harold turns his attention
back to his youngest child. The little one drops a boat with
a big splash and sings about how his friend the bullfrog
"always had some mighty fine wine". Harold uses a washcloth
on his neck.

The muffled conversation in the other room comes to an end as
the receiver clicks back into place. After several long
moments, Sarah appears in the door of the bathroom and leans
against the door jamb. Very quietly, she is crying.

Harold looks up at his wife.

FADE TO BLACK.

The MUSIC BEGINS, loud and strong. Like all the music which
follows, it is high-energy, move-those-feet, Sixties rock 'n
roll.

FADE UP AS THE MAIN TITLE BEGINS. We begin to INTERCUT:

2   INT. ROOM - DAY   2

ALEX GETTING DRESSED I. (All Extreme Close-ups.)
A suit pant leg, neatly pressed, pulled over a tanned calf.

3   INT. KITCHEN, KAREN'S HOUSE (BLOOMFIELD HILLS, MICHIGAN) - DAY 3

Full screen close-up of KAREN'S face. Immediately we begin
widening to include her environment, a lavishly and recently
remodeled kitchen, all dark-grained cabinets and gleaming tiles.
Karen, very pretty in her tennis whites, sits at the butcher-
block center island, a telephone next to the coffee cup she's
staring into. Behind her, through a window, a large, neat

                                                   CONTINUED:

suburban lawn turning brown in the Michigan fall, the surround-   3
ing trees bleakly denuded. A Maid, wearing her whites, passes
through the kitchen.

4   INT. ROOM - DAY   4

ALEX GETTING DRESSED II: A crisply starched shirt gets
buttoned up the chest by strong male fingers.

5   INT. BEDROOM, MICHAEL'S APARTMENT (NEW YORK CITY) - DAY   5

MICHAEL'S face. Immediately begin widening to take in the
room and Annie, Michael's girlfriend, a black woman. She is
filling Michael's well-worn overnight bag with his clothes
from the closet. Michael's eyes dart frantically about his
messy desk as he searches for something and keeps up a steady,
hyped-up monologue we cannot hear. Annie folds a dark tie
into the bag and comes up next to Michael. Very calmly, she
extracts a new package of batteries from the debris of the
desk and places them in Michael's hand. This stops him cold
and calms him down, as she always does. He enfolds her in
his arms, sadly. She soothes him.

6   INT. ROOM - DAY   6

ALEX GETTING DRESSED III: The shiny buckle of a dress belt
is fastened over the buttons of the suit pants.

7   INT. MEG'S LAW OFFICE, SKYSCRAPER (ATLANTA, GEORGIA) - DAY 7

MEG'S face. Her eyes, too, flick over the papers which will
soon come into view on her large, immaculate desk. But these
eyes are different from Michael's. For one thing, their move-
ments are steady, concise, controlled. Secondly, they are
very red from a long and recent cry.

Meg sets some papers neatly into the open briefcase on her
credenza, looks at them a beat, then lights up a cigarette
and stands gazing over the briefcase at the Atlanta skyline.
The office is large and carefully appointed; her view is a
good one.

8   INT. ROOM - DAY   8

ALEX GETTING DRESSED IV: A shiny black oxford is tightly
knotted on a black-stockinged foot. A man's finger rubs at
a single scuff.

9   INT. FIRST CLASS SECTION, 747 - SAM'S SEAT - DAY   9

SAM'S face. He looks up, his handsome features in a mild
alchoholic daze. The Stewardess, a stack of magazines in
hand, is flirting with him aggressively. He smiles over a
row of empty little vodka bottles. She teases a moment more,
then reveals the cover of the top magazine with a flourish:

it is US Magazine and on the cover is a smiling-shot of Sam.   9
The man himself seems slightly jolted by his mirror image at
this unsuspecting moment. But he recovers quickly and charmingly
indicates to the Stewardess what he wants right now -- not her,
not the magazine, but another little vodka bottle to empty.

10   INT. ROOM - DAY   10

ALEX GETTING DRESSED V: A woman's sleek fingers have made a
neat knot in a conservative tie. Now they slide the knot
lovingly, almost sensually, up to the collar.

11   INT. LIVING ROOM, THE SUMMER HOUSE (CAROLINA SHORE) - DAY   11

CHLOE'S face, seems very young. All the others have been in
their early 30's, but Chloe is barely past twenty and there's
no question about the difference it makes. This face, this
young, smooth, striking face, is straining now, heavily beaded
with sweat. Chloe is on the thick carpet of this luxurious
room doing tortuous dancer stretches. Her long, wonderful,
generous body is bent at an impossible angle. She is working
hard.

The room is singular to say the least, done entirely and
expensively in original Art Deco furnishings. Chloe's bright
leotard jumps extravagantly from the overall muted color scheme.

This house belongs to Sarah and Harold.

12   INT. ROOM - DAY   12

ALEX GETTING DRESSED VI: A brush pulls his thick hair neatly
away from a part. One more touch makes it perfect.

13   INT./EXT. NICK'S PORSCHE (ON THE ROAD) - DAY   13

No face this time. Rather, we have NICK'S hands on the steering
wheel of his aging 911. Beyond the hands, we can see the scenery
streaking by at a rate inconsistent with a lawful speed. That
impression is reinforced by the MUSIC, which now seems to have
been emanating all along from the tape deck of this car, blasting
it forward through the countryside. Now his right hand disappears
for a second and when it reappears we follow it to the ashtray,
where it stubs out a massive joint and leaves the roach, then
travels to the glove compartment. From the mess of that box it
extracts a large bottle of pills and flips the cap off with a
thumb. The hand shakes a dozen pills of various colors on the
passenger seat. The fingers forage through pills, picking out
only white ones. The hand disappears from view.

We're outside and behind the Porsche now, trying to keep up.
But suddenly the car jumps into hyperspace, and is gone.

Taking the MUSIC with it.

14   INT. ROOM - DAY   14

ALEX GETTING DRESSED VII: It's very quiet now. Only the rustling of the shirt's broadcloth, as the sleek feminine fingers pull a cuff down out of the shadow of the suit's sleeve. The fingers turn the arm, which seems oddly slack, and insert a cuff-link into the holes of the cuff. Then, very deliberately, first on one hand, then the other, the fingers pull the cuffs down, to cover that which body make-up could not hide -- the straight, awful slits across the tender insides of the wrists.

THE MAIN TITLE ENDS.

15   EXT.   CHURCH (CAROLINA SHORE) - DAY   15

People are arriving for Alex's funeral. It's not a huge crowd
but the small parking area is busy. Near the entry drive, next
to the parked hearse and limos, stands Harold, directing traffic,
as much from nervous energy as actual need. A cab pulls in.
Sam gets out with a single bag and pays the driver. Harold comes
over and embraces Sam. It is the first of many ambivalent
reunions today; they're glad to see each other, but desperately
unhappy about the cause.

                         SAM
          Harold.

                         HAROLD
          Sam.

They hold each other at arms length.

                         SAM
          Christ.

Harold just nods. Harold picks up Sam's bag and carries it
across the drive to his big Mercedes.

                         HAROLD
          I'll put it in here. You can drive
          this to the cemetary.

Sam stops on the work "cemetary".

                         SAM
          Christ. Were you here?

                         HAROLD
          No, Alex was staying here at the summer
          house. Sarah and I were at the Richmond
          place with the kids.

INT. SANCTUARY

Chloe sits all alone in the front row on the left side of
the sanctuary as the rows behind her fill up. She looks
calm and

                                                    CONTINUED:

beautiful in a second-hand print dress and boots. With dry, 23
clear eyes, she watches Alex's coffin being wheeled onto the
altar. Alex's Parents move in to the front row across the aisle.
Alex's Mother casts one killing glance in Chloe's direction
before her husband steps into her eyeline and gets her seated.

AT THE DOOR OF THE SANCTUARY. Harold points Karen and Richard
toward seats on the far right side, next to the organ on which
a Church Organist has just begun to play "Rock of Ages". An
Usher hovers nearby. As Sam and Michael come in, Harold indicates to the Usher that these two are pallbearers. The Usher
nods and starts to lead them toward the front rows on the left.
Harold takes Michael's arm and walks with him.

>   HAROLD
>   I want you to sit with Chloe.

>   MICHAEL
>   Okay.

>   HAROLD
>   I've got to be up there, and it's a
>   little touchy with Alex's folks.

>   MICHAEL
>   I understand.

Harold gives him a "I knew you would" squeeze.

>   MICHAEL
>   Who's Chloe?

Harold gestures discreetly in Chloe's direction.

>   HAROLD
>   It's Alex's girlfriend.

Michael peers into the pews.

Harold indicates Chloe in the front row, which they have almost
reached. Michael is impressed, brightening at the sight of her.
But when he speaks to Harold, he's all solicitous friend.

>   MICHAEL
>   I'll take care of her.

Michael moves off toward her as Harold climbs onto the altar
and takes a seat next to the MINISTER who greets him comfortingly.

AT THE BACK OF THE SANCTUARY, Sarah waves off the Usher and
starts down the aisle with Meg. Suddenly Meg stops at a rear
aisle seat behind and away from the crowd. Sarah indicates
seats near the front left side (where Sam has sat) but Meg

declines, wishing a measure of solitude. Sarah goes down to
the front and sits next to Alex's Parents, who treat her like
a daughter.

MEG'S FACE. She takes in the scene sadly. Then focuses up ahead.

WHAT SHE SEES: For several beats she lingers on Alex's coffin,
then, through a jumble of heads, she sees Michael leaning close
to Chloe, murmuring his comfort. Chloe is impassive. Meg's
gaze shifts back a row on the far left and settles on Sam. Sam
is staring intently off across the sanctuary. Meg follows his
look. He is staring at Karen.

AT KAREN. She fidgets with the paper memorial program and looks
up, across the church. There is an instant of flustered panic
as her eyes lock with Sam. She seems momentarily guilty about
Richard, then nods at Sam and half-waves. Sam nods back and
shifts his attentions to Richard, who he finds staring at him.

THE ORGAN MUSIC STOPS. The MINISTER, a balding, white-haired
old gentleman moves slowly to the pulpit with feeble, hesitant
steps. He speaks with a thick Carolina drawl.

                    MINISTER
          Sometimes it is hard for us to believe
          that the Good Lord has a plan ...

Meg shakes her head. This is going to be just what she feared.
She murmurs to herself, ahead of the Minister --

                    MEG
                (sotto voice)
          ... and this is one of those times.

                    MINISTER
          ... this is one of those times. I
          didn't know Alex Marshall personally ...

                    MEG
                (sotto voice)
          ... but that won't stop me from shooting
          off my mouth about him.

                    MINISTER
          ... but after speaking with his loved
          ones, I feel as though I did.

Chloe watches the Minister blankly. Michael can't help himself;
he watches Chloe, eyes flicking over her relentlessly.

Alex's Mother is find this part of the Minister's speech
especially painful. Sarah takes her hand.

                         MINISTER
          ... a brilliant physics student at the
          University of Michigan who, paradoxically,
          chose to turn his back on science and
          taste of life through a seemingly random
          series of occupations. Just one of many
          paradoxes in too brief a journey.

                                              CONTINUED:

                                      With his next utterance
we notice that some tiny little change has happened to his tone.
It comes in so quietly and subtly that the crowd is a little
slow to notice it. Or recognize immediately what it is --
pure, jolting, white-hot anger.

                         MINISTER
              I'm afraid I can find no easy comfort
              here today. When a man like Alex
              <u>chooses</u> to leave us, something is
              <u>very wrong</u> in the world ...

26   EXT. CHURCH   26

The Porsche skids to a stop at the curb behind the limos, the
blasting MUSIC dies with the engine. Nick jumps out and hustles
toward the church, knotting a tie as he goes. He's wearing an
old corduroy jacket and blue jeans, his only outfit. The Drivers
watch him disappear and eye his filthy car.

27   INT. SANCTUARY   27

Now Meg is <u>really</u> <u>listening</u> to the Minister; she's surprised and
intrigued by what she's hearing.

                         MINISTER
              ... if young people--capable of so
              much good--can destroy themselves.
              <u>Now</u>, when the need for them in our
              troubled world has never been greater!...

Behind Meg, we see Nick enter the sanctuary. The Usher immediately intercepts him and the two men whisper together. Having
identified Nick as another pallbearer, the Usher points him down
to the left front (where Sam is seated). Nick heads that way,
stopping only long enough to touch Meg on her shoulder. Meg
looks up, smiles sadly and puts her hand momentarily on his.

From his seat on the altar, Harold watches Nick move to his seat.
He's glad to see him.

Karen sees Nick make his way to Sam. Something strong flicks

                                                        CONTINUED:

through her eyes.   Richard turns to look at the newcomer
curiously.

Nick sits down next to Sam.   They clasp hands warmly.

The Minister leans over the pulpit now.   His voice is softer
now, but awesomely intense.

                         MINISTER
                   (indicating the coffin)
          ... But why are we left with this?
          It makes me angry. And I don't know
          what to do with my anger... Are not
          the satisfactions of being a good man
          among our common men great enough to
          sustain us any more? Where did Alex's
          hope go?

                                              CONTINUED

The Minister pauses. Sarah stares at him as if mesmerized.

Meg doesn't know that tears are streaming down her cheeks.

> MINISTER
> Maybe that is the small resolution we
> can take from here today ... to try
> and regain that hope which must have
> eluded Alex.
>   (long pause, then softly)
> Let us all try to have hope.

The Minister bows his head a moment then turns to Harold.

> MINISTER
> Harold.

Harold just stares at him a moment, then seems to remember and
stands up. The Minister sits down as Harold approaches the pulpit, pulling an index card full of notes from his pocket. He
stands there staring at the index card a little while. Finally
he looks up. There are tears in his eyes. The notes are of
no use to him now.

Nick and Sam and Michael all stare up at him and they are all
stricken now by the sight of Harold's face. That, more than
anything, has made this event real to them at last.

> HAROLD
>   (with some difficulty)
> I did know Alex. And I loved him ...
> I see here today all those people that
> Alex loved ... His family ... his
> friends ...
>   (he has to stop for a moment)
> ... Not all of us have been able to see
> each other much these last years. But
> neither time nor distance could break
> the bonds we feel ... Alex drew us
> together from the start and now ... he
> brings us together again.

Karen's body is quietly shaking as she cries. Richard puts an
arm around her.

> HAROLD
>   (after a long silence)
> I don't know why this happened ... but
> I do know that there was always some-
> thing about Alex that was ... too
> good ... for this world. I only hope
> that wherever he is now ... he ...

Harold breaks down completely now. He can't go on. The Minister
comes forward and leads Harold gently back to his seat, then

CONTINUED:

returns to the pulpit. He reads from a sheet of paper on the pulpit.

Sarah watches, pained but dry-eyed. She comforts Alex's Mother.

                         MINISTER
              Burial will be at the Westglade Memorial
              Park. There will be a reception at the
              home of Harold and Sarah Cooper, 23
              Bayside Road, immediately following.
              Now Karen Bowers, an old college friend
              of Alex's will play one of Alex's favorite
              songs.

Karen leaves her seat by Richard and replaces the Organist as the church becomes very quiet. She checks the organ pedals, sets herself and begins to play: it takes a few bars to recognize it on this instrument, but the song she is playing is a hard-driving, kick-out-the-jams, rock classic of the sixties. Some of the older Mourners exchange concerned looks, but Alex's friends cannot suppress small, pleased smiles of recognition and memory.

EXT. CHURCH - FRONT DOORS - DAY

The organ music continues.

As the casket reaches the front doors, the Funeral Director stops the procession. From here, down the steps to the hearse, the coffin must be carried.

AT THE HEARSE, the Pallbearers slide the casket into the back, each of their hands in turn coming off the handles, empty, as they let go.

AT THE CARS. The Mourners have spilled outside and are making their way to the cars.

                                              CONTINUED:

Nick embraces Sarah warmly. She moves off to the first limo,   28
which she enters with Alex's Parents. Harold hugs Nick and
follows Sarah.

Sam gives Karen a hug and is introduced to Richard. Nick steps
up and gets the same treatment.

Michael has renewed his custody of Chloe. Sam points the way
and the three of them walk over to Harold's Mercedes. Michael
opens the back door decorously for Chloe, but she seems not to
notice, going around instead to take the passenger seat. Michael
gets in back alone. Sam drives.

Nick has Meg protectively under his arm as he leads her to his
Porsche and opens the passenger door for her. She's feeling
better already in her good friend's presence. She sits down,
but immediately arches her rear off the seat and sweeps a hand-
ful of pills from the seat into her palm. Nick apologizes for
the mess, takes and pockets the pills.

Richard, talking up a storm, wheels their rented car into the
line of the cortege as Karen watches the crowd silently from
the passenger seat.

A Motorcycle Cop in the lead, the procession snakes out of the
church parking lot.

29   EXT.   THE TRIP TO THE CEMETARY (VARIOUS SHOTS) - DAY   29

The funeral procession moves uninterrupted through the pretty,
little resort community. Now in the off-season, this beach
town is largely deserted. Only a few cars must wait at inter-
sections for the passing cortege, which glides through a park,
along beachfront, then around the small bay to the beat of the
rock MUSIC.

We INTERCUT this progression with:

30   INT. MERCEDES   30

Michael is leaning forward between the two front seats as far
as possible. Sam looks past him, over at Chloe.

                    SAM
          Are you alright?

                    CHLOE
          Yeah. I'm a little disappointed.
                    (indicates the limos ahead)
          I wanted to ride up there.

Michael and Sam understand; they're sympathetic.

                    CHLOE
          I've always wanted to ride in a limo.

                                                        CONTINUED:

Michael and Sam exchange looks.   30

> MICHAEL
> I do half my work in limos.

> CHLOE
> Are you a chauffeur?

Sam laughs.

> MICHAEL
> No. I'm a journalist.

This, too, draws a laugh from Sam. Michael shoots him an
irritated glance.

> MICHAEL
> I write for <u>People</u> Magazine.

Sam smiles. Michael sees it.

> MICHAEL
> (to Sam)
> I can't believe you're still mad about
> that thing.

> SAM
> Michael, this isn't the time. Let's
> forget it.

> MICHAEL
> I will if you will. On this day most
> of all we should remember we're friends.

Sam nods. Michael nods.

> CHLOE
> (to Sam)
> And you're an actor?

Sam affirms it. Now Michael can't stop himself -- he snorts a
laugh. Sam shoots him a look.

31   INT. PORSCHE   31

Meg takes a deep toke from a large joint.

> NICK
> (warning)
> That's pretty strong stuff.

> MEG
> I feel terrible ... I had a fight with
> Alex the last time we spoke. I yelled
> at him.

                                NICK
                That's probably why he killed himself.   31

She looks at him now.

                                MEG
                Good ol' Nick.

He smiles, touches her. They drive in silence.

                                NICK
                             (finally)
                What was the fight about?

She remembers, ruefully, through the marijuana haze.

                                MEG
                I told him he was wasting his life.

33 INT. RICHARD'S RENTED CAR   33

    Karen stares silently ahead. Richard can't get over it --

                                RICHARD
                ... I mean nothing like you described.
                Not at all. Not one of them looks the
                way I thought they would. I can't
                believe these are the same people you've
                been talking about all these years.
                Really.

    Karen stews. Richard laughs at a thought.

                                RICHARD
                I'd love to hear the way you described
                me to them.

34 INT. HEARSE   34

    The casket rocks gently.

35 EXT. CEMETARY - DAY   35

    The MUSIC ends as the cortege makes its way into the cemetary.

36 EXT. CEMETARY ROAD   36

    The Porsche pulls to its stopping place in the line. Meg has
    only a tiny roach left. Nick takes it from her fingers and stubs
    it in the ashtray. Before he's finished, Meg has opened the door

                                                                    CONTINUED:

and moved off across the cemetary. Nick hurries around the car
and quickly catches up to Meg, taking hold of her. She's con-
fused. Nick points out that she has started in the wrong direction. He turns her around and leads her toward Alex's gravesite.

EXT. GRAVESITE

Later. Alex's coffin, surrounded by flowers. The Mourners
are crowded in tightly around it.

EXT. THE SUMMER HOUSE - DAY

Sarah's and Harold's Summer House is a huge, beautifully main-
tained Victorian with wide, wrap-around verandahs. The street
around the manicured lawn is crowded with the parked cars of the
Mourners. Some of the reception guests have overflowed onto the
porch despite the crisp fall weather.

INT. DINING ROOM

This is the same house we glimpsed during Chloe's exercise in
the title sequence and the whole interior is done with the same
affluent care as the Art Deco living room we saw then.

The crowd is noisy, lively even. There is enormous relief to
have the funeral behind them and the gathering could easily
be mistaken for a happier occasion. Michael has loaded his
plate from a bounteous buffet and stands with Nick, who eyes
the food, but continues to merely drink.

                    MICHAEL
          Amazing tradition. They throw a great
          party for you on the one day they know
          you can't come.

INT. LIVING ROOM

Meg and Sarah are together in the living room. Sarah is staring
off into the den at Chloe with a look of distaste.

                    MEG
          How long were they together?

                    SARAH
          Four months.
                    (shakes her head)
          I can't believe it. His funeral and
          she's stoned.

Meg gets a headache, instantly.

Richard and Michael are sitting on the stairs, eating.

                         RICHARD
              Karen and I are staying here tonight.
              We have a flight back to Detroit in
              the morning. Are you staying?

                         MICHAEL
              No. I have to fly out to Dallas
              tonight. I'm interviewing a four-
              teen year old, blind baton twirler.

                         RICHARD
              Where do you get those stories from?

                         MICHAEL
              It's just good, investigative journalism.

INT. LIVING ROOM

Karen and Sam stand together, slightly uneasy.

                         SAM
              How's your life?

                         KAREN
              Great. How about you?

                         SAM
              Not so great.

                         KAREN
              <u>Oh</u>, we're telling the truth.

Sam smiles. They understand each other.

                         SAM
              You heard I got divorced?

She certainly did. A ten year old BOY FAN comes up next to
Sam. He has a Memorial Program and pen in hand.

                         BOY FAN
                    (to Sam)
              Are you J.T. Lancer?

                         SAM
                    (friendly)
              That's the character I play. I'm
              Sam Weber.

                         BOY FAN
              Well, can I have your autograph, whoever
              you are?

                                                   CONTINUED:

Sam puts a hand on the boy's shoulder.

                    SAM
          Don't you think this a time for us
          to be thinking about Alex?

                    BOY FAN
          I'll give you a buck.

                    SAM
          You're on!

Karen laughs.

INT.   DINING ROOM

Sarah takes a tray of food from one of the Hired Help and
starts arranging it on the buffet. Karen and Michael are
with her. Karen surveys the crowd.

                    KAREN
          You'd never get a crowd this big at
          my funeral.

                    MICHAEL
          Ah, Karen ... I'll come. And I'll
          bring a date.

                    KAREN
               (to Sarah)
          I know this is hard for you, but it's
          all beautiful.

                    SARAH
          Yeah, we put on a great funeral here.

                    MICHAEL
          Maybe I'll have mine here too.

                    SARAH
               (continues to work)
          We give first preference to people who
          kill themselves in one of our bathrooms.

Even Michael is stopped by this. He and Karen look at Sarah.
She continues to arrange the food.

                    SARAH
          That was a terrible thing to say. I
          don't know why I said that.

Michael puts his arm around her.

Meg, very stoned, is wedged as securely as possible against
a post on the railing. Sam has brought her a plate of food.
He holds it for her.

                    MEG
      ... that's why I never smoke anymore.
      Dope makes me stupid.

Nick has walked up on this.

                    NICK
      You talking about me?

                    MEG
      There's the guy that did this to me.
            (she puts her arm around Nick)
      I no longer know how to handle myself
      stoned.

                    NICK
      You don't have to "handle yourself"
      with us.

Meg knows it true. She embraces Nick.

                    MEG
      Will you marry me?

Sam gestures towards himself.

                    MEG
      Both of you?

INT. HALLWAY

Michael has got Sam cornered in a private spot.

                  MICHAEL
      ... I don't know where they got that
      shit about your marriage from. I
      didn't even know they were doing a
      story on you. I don't know why you
      don't believe me.

                    SAM
      Let's drop it.

                  MICHAEL
      Tell me you believe me.

                    SAM
      I believe you. I always believe you.

                            CONTINUED:

                         MICHAEL
          Good. Honest to god, Sam, I know it's
          crap. That's why I'm getting out.

                         SAM
          Yeah?   What are you going to do?

                         MICHAEL
          I'm opening a club.

                         SAM
          No shit.

                         MICHAEL
          Yeah. Like Elaine's. But hipper, you
          know. Elaine's is dead.

                         SAM
          You've got the money?

                         MICHAEL
          Almost ... almost.

                         SAM
          Well, let me know.

                         MICHAEL
          ... er, what do you mean?

                         SAM
          I might be interested.

Sam walks away. Michael watches him go, his mind whirring like
a calculator.

INT. DEN

The crowd is gone now, but Chloe is sitting in exactly the
same spot. Karen sits with her. They're both drinking.

                         KAREN
          So you and Alex were staying here?

                         CHLOE
          Yeah. We have a room downstairs. We
          did ... I do.
                    (a beat)
          I found him.

Karen winces.

                         KAREN
          It must have been awful.

                              CHLOE
                Yeah, it was a real mess.

Karen looks at her.

                              KAREN
                What are you going to do now?

                              CHLOE
                Oh, we cleaned it up.

Karen tries to stay with her.

                              KAREN
                So ... you're going to stay here?

                              CHLOE
                Yeah. For a while. 'Till Sarah
                kicks me out.

                              KAREN
                I'm sure she'd never do that.

Chloe shrugs, takes a drink.

INT.   UPSTAIRS HALL

Michael sits at a table in the quiet hall. Michael listens
to the phone at his ear, until --

                              MICHAEL
                Give me a break here, Jim. I'll fly
                out to Dallas on Monday. She's not
                gonna regain her eyesight over the
                weekend.
                          (he listens)
                I'm telling you I think I've got some-
                thing good right here.
                          (he listens, then begins to vamp)
                I don't know ... It's about everything --
                suicide, despair. Where did our hope go?
                Lost hope. That's it, lost hope.
                          (he listens)
                You think everything's boring. You
                wouldn't say that if it was the Lost
                Hope Diet.

EXT.   STREET IN FRONT OF HOUSE/FRONT WALK - DAY

Harold and Sarah exchange long goodbyes with Alex's Parents
and see them on their way. Harold takes Sarah's arm as they
start up the walk. Sarah leans on Harold.

                              HAROLD
              Michael's office called and he doesn't
              have to be in Dallas until Monday. He
              asked me if he could stay the weekend.

                              SARAH
              Harold, you didn't ...

                              HAROLD
              What could I say? He know Sam is
              staying ... and Richard and Karen,
              and Meg.

                              SARAH
              Meg's not staying.

                              HAROLD
              Well, actually...

Sarah gets his drift. She's not happy about it, but she's
not sure what she feels. She's tired.

                              SARAH
              Where are we going to put everybody?

They start up the verandah stairs.

                              HAROLD
              We'll make room.

Nick is leaning against a post at the top of the stairs,
a glass in hand.

                              NICK
                  Hi, guys.

Harold and Sarah look up at him. They love him. They look at
each other.

EXT. DRIVEWAY - DUSK

Nick has pulled the Porsche next to the house and is lying
under it with his lower body sticking out. He's messing
with something under the car. Richard stands above him
admiring the car, despite its ragged condition.

                              RICHARD
              ... Yeah, advertising's all right.
              There's a lot of bullshit with clients
              and stuff, but it's all right. And
                              (MORE)

                    RICHARD (CONT'D)
          it's a decent living -- not as much
          as we spend, of course.

Richard laughs, painfully. Nick tries to chuckle from below.

                    RICHARD
          Just kidding ... It's <u>exactly</u> as much
          as we spend.
                    (almost another laugh)
          What d'ya got there, oil leak or some-
          thing? Can I give you a hand?

                    NICK
          No ... I think I've got it.

He slides out from under the car and stands up. In one hand is
a wrench. In the other, a very·neat, plastic-wrapped package,
about book size -- obviously a large, dealer-size quantity of
some illegal narcotic.

54   INT.   DAUGHTER'S BEDROOM - DUSK   54

Karen and Sarah are making up the twin beds in the cheerfully
decorated bedroom of Sarah's six year-old daughter.

                    KAREN
          ... I feel like I've never been alone
          in my own home. Never. Either Richard
          is there or the boys or the housekeeper.
          Remember those lab rats that went nuts
          when they were deprived of their privacy?

                    SARAH
          <u>They're</u> living with you too?!
                    (Karen laughs)
          Should we push these beds together?

                    KAREN
          Why?

                    SARAH
                    (a look)
          O-kay ... how 'bout further apart?

INT.   ATTIC - DUSK

The attic is a large, clean, unfinished room up under the sloping,
gabled roof. There are two twin beds up here, some furniture
and lots of neatly-packed old things. Harold and Sam are making

                                        CONTINUED:

up the beds.

                    HAROLD
     ... In January we open in Greensboro
     and in April our second store in Norfolk.

                    SAM
     How many is that?

                    HAROLD
     Twenty-seven and twenty-eight.

                    SAM
          (whistles)
     You better watch out, some big monster
     is gonna buy you.

                    HAROLD
     We've had offers.

Sam works a moment, shakes his head.

                    SAM
     Who would have thought we'd both
     make so much bread? Two revolu-
     tionaries.

                    HAROLD
     Yeah.
          (a beat)
     Good thing it's not important to
     us.

                    SAM
     Right.

They laugh, get back to work.

                    SAM
     Fuck'em if they can't take a joke.

Harold laughs again.

56   EXT. OUTSIDE GROUND FLOOR - CHLOE'S DOOR - DUSK   * 56

Michael knocks on a door.   *

                    MICHAEL
     Chloe? Are you there?

Chloe opens the door. She is wearing a tee shirt and bikini
panties and looks irresistible.

                    CHLOE
     Yeah?

CONTINUED:

56 CONTINUED: -25-   56

                              MICHAEL
                        (regaining his breath)
                  Hi. I just wanted to make sure you
                  were all right.

                              CHLOE
                  I'm fine.

Michael stands there, looking at her.

                              MICHAEL
                  Good.

                              CHLOE
                  Thanks, Michael.

She closes the door. He is slow to leave, transported by the
sound of his name on her lips, a lifting of the spirits re-
flected in the first beats of the rock MUSIC that begins now
and continues over --

THE UNPACKING MONTAGE:

57   INT. ATTIC - DUSK   57

Sam opens his fashionably worn-out, very expensive leather bag
and takes out: several identically faded, carefully-pressed
work shirts and jeans; a beeper from a phone-mate, three TV
scripts with "J. T. LANCER" slashed across them, a Nikon, a
paperback, THE PORTABLE KAFKA, and a hairdryer.

58   INT. DAUGHTER'S BEDROOM - DUSK   58

Karen opens the huge suitcase on her bed and begins unloading
the top items: a huge make-up selection case; a diaphragm;
a copy of US Magazine with Sam on the cover; a hairdryer and
curling iron. Underneath all this is an enormous amount of
clothes.

Richard makes an artful arrangement on his bedside table of two
items: a bottle of Maalox and a traveling picture of their two
sons, eight and ten years old.

59   INT. HAROLD AND SARAH'S SON'S ROOM - DUSK   59

Michael unpacks and sets up camp. He takes out: a mini-
cassette tape recorder; a reporter's note-book; a harmonica;
a hairdryer; some bright bikini undershorts. Some prophylactics
fall out of the clothing. He stuffs them back in his bag.

60   EXT. DRIVEWAY - DUSK   60 *

Nick opens the trunk of the Porsche. He has no suitcase. His
clothes and toiletries are a jumble in the trunk. He picks
through it.

                                                        CONTINUED:

Harold comes out of the house in running gear -- extremely   60
well-used -- says something to Nick and heads off into the
gloom for a serious run.

61   INT. MAID'S ROOM   61

Meg stands at the dresser on top of which she has set her legal
briefcase. She stares at the crucifix hanging on the wall above
the dresser. Finally, she flips open the top of the briefcase,
blocking out the sight of the crucifix. The MUSIC FADES.

62   INT. MASTER BEDROOM - SHOWER   62

Hot water is beating down, steaming the room, but there doesn't
appear to be anyone in the shower. Now we hear a HUMAN SOUND
in the roar of the water. Now we see Sarah -- she is sitting
on the floor of the shower. The water beats down on her, making
it impossible to see her tears as she cries.

63   INT. LIVING ROOM - NIGHT   63

LATER. Meg, Sam, Karen and Michael sit rather stiffly nursing
drinks. Meg wears a borrowed robe and fluffy slippers. Wonderful, mellow Sixties MOTOWN MUSIC plays softly from the elaborate
stereo system.

                         MEG
              ... So here I was working with the
              Philadelphia public defenders and my
              clients were just the scum of the
              earth, really extreme repulsivos.
              I mean one of my guys got caught in
              the house, right, and he and his
              friends have beat up the husband
              and raped the wife and then tried
              to blow the whole place up. And I
              asked him what happened and he says,
              "I was in Montreal at the time."   *

                         MICHAEL
              Who did you think your clients were
              going to be? Grumpy and Sneezy?

                         SAM
              No, Huey and Bobby.

                         MEG
              I don't know. I just didn't think
              they'd all be so ... guilty.

Harold comes in, freshly showered and feeling good. He walks
up behind the sofa Meg's on and does a neat Fosbury Flop to

land prone on the sofa beside her. Michael and Sam seem relieved 6:
by his behavior model in this fancy room. Michael immediately
puts his feet up on the coffee table; Sam swivels to lie down
on the sofa.

> SAM
>
> And then?

> MEG
>
> And then ... I left. I had a friend
> from law school who was with a firm
> in Atlanta doing real-estate law. I
> went to see them. And the offices
> seemed so clean. And the clients were
> raping only the land. And, of course,
> there was the money. El greedo strikes
> again.

She takes Harold's feet on her lap in a friendly way.

> HAROLD
>
> Sarah has a robe like that.

> MEG
>
> Not this weekend she doesn't.

> HAROLD
>
> I always want to jump her when she
> wears that thing.

> MICHAEL
>
> Harold, don't you have any other
> music? Like from this century.

> HAROLD
>
> There is no other music. Not in
> my house.

> MICHAEL
>
> There's been a lot of terrific music
> in the last ten years.

> HAROLD
> (totally uninterested)
>
> Like what?

Sarah settles onto the arm of the sofa near Harold's head. She's
in a robe and has a drink in hand and looks much healthier for
having cried. Michael passes a smoking joint to Sam after Meg
waves it off.

> KAREN
>
> How about you, Michael? Tell us about
> big time journalism.

                              MICHAEL
          Where I work we have only one edi-
          torial rule: you can't write any-
          thing longer than the average person
          can read during the average crap.
          I'm tired of having all my work read
          in the can.

                              HAROLD
          People read Tolstoy in the can.

                              MICHAEL
          Yeah, but they can't finish it.

Sarah surveys the lounging group.

                              SARAH
          This is certainly a familiar scene.

They know what she means.

                              SAM
          It's making me feel very guilty. I'm
          so happy to here and I'm sick about
          the reason.

                              SARAH
                    (gets up)
          I'm going to bed.

                              SAM
          I'm sorry. We'll talk about something
          else.

                              SARAH
          That's okay. I'm exhausted. Goodnight,
          everyone.

They say goodnight as she heads out with her drink.

                              HAROLD
          I'll be up in a minute.

                              SAM
                    (to Harold)
          I'm sorry.

                              HAROLD
          Hey, we all feel that way.

                              SAM
          I'd forgotten what this is like. In
          L.A. I don't know who to trust. I
          feel like everybody wants something
          from me. I know that sounds terrible,
          but it's true ...

                                            CONTINUED:

                              MEG   * 63
                         (understands)   *
          Tell me about it. It's a cold   *
          world out there. Sometimes I   *
          think I'm getting a little frosty   *
          myself.   *

                                         CONTINUED:

CONTINUED:

Karen watches Sam, rapt.

                        SAM
            ... I don't know what people think
            of me. Or why they like me, or even
            <u>if</u> they like me.

There is a rather long, pregnant pause.

                        HAROLD
            You don't have that problem here. You
            <u>know</u> I don't like you.

                        MICHAEL
            Me either.

                        MEG
            Ditto.

Meg gets up and walks out. Sam laughs.

64   INT. ATTIC - NIGHT   64

Nick snorts a line of cocaine on the dresser top, straightens
and pockets his paraphernalia. As he turns to leave, Meg comes
up the stairs from the second floor and blocks his way.

                        NICK
            I was just coming down.

                        MEG
            Don't.

She takes his hand and leads him over to one of the beds.

                        NICK
            What are we doing?

                        MEG
            I didn't get a chance to talk to you
            before. You got me stoned too quick.

She sits him down. Then drops the robe off her body as she
talks. Underneath she is wearing a long nightshirt, knee
socks and the fluffy slippers; it's an unusual idea of sexy.

                        MEG
            I'm okay now. I'm just drunk. And
            therefore brave.

She sits on his lap and puts her arms around him.

                        NICK
            I've always been a cowardly drunk
            myself.

It's Harold, Sam, Karen and Michael now.

> HAROLD
> ... I bought the land three years ago.
> There's an old house there. Alex and
> Chloe were working on it. It's a pretty
> spot. I could take you out there tomorrow
> if you like.

He is silent for a moment.

> HAROLD
> That's what I don't get. One of the
> things I don't get. He was really
> involved in that. I went with him
> three weeks ago to buy a table saw.
> Why does he do a thing like that?

They are all quiet for several beats.

> SAM
> I should have known.

> KAREN
> How could you know?

> HAROLD
> No one knew. I can't even believe it
> now.

> SAM
> I don't care. I should have known.

INT.   ATTIC - NIGHT

Nick and Meg are still sitting on the bed. Meg is on
Nick's lap, embracing him.

> MEG
> All I want is a little warmth.

> NICK
> (holding her, easing her off his lap)
> Meg, sweetheart, did I ever tell you
> what happened to me in Vietnam?

INT.   LIVING ROOM - NIGHT

It's still Harold, Sam, Karen and Michael.

Suddenly, there are a woman's hysterical SCREAMS from
upstairs. They jump up and run toward the steps.

66   INT.   SECOND FLOOR HALL/BOTTOM OF ATTIC STEPS - NIGHT   66

Sarah is halfway up the attic steps as the group from the living
room arrives. Meg stumbles down the steps toward them, struggling
into the flannel robe, near hysterical.

>   MEG
>   There's a fucking bat up there! I
>   think it touched my hair.

On hearing this, Harold relaxes a bit and heads down the hall
toward a closet. Karen backs away. Sarah laughs.

>   KAREN
>   Yech. I hate them. They're like
>   rats with wings.

>   MICHAEL
>   No, pigeons are rats with wings.

>   SARAH
>   They're harmless. They eat the
>   mosquitoes.

>   MEG
>   (heading for her room)
>   I'm going to wash my hair and puke.

>   MICHAEL
>   (calling after her)
>   Puke first.

>   SAM
>   (to Sarah)
>   Stand aside.

He goes up.

>   MICHAEL
>   I'll cover your rear.

CONTINUED:

He stays with Sarah. Harold returns with a broom in hand. He   66
mounts the stairs humming the theme from "Raiders of the Lost
Ark" --

                         HAROLD
               Dah-duh-dah-dah-dum-de-dah.

67 INT. ATTIC - NIGHT   67

Nick is swatting at the fluttering black spot as it whips back
and forth across the room. Sam watches from the relative pro-
tection of the stairwell. When he makes out Nick's weapon he
panics -- it's his sweater.

                         SAM
               Hey. That's cashmere!

Harold comes up past Sam, his broom at the ready. The bat
disappears into the gloom at the far end of the attic and doesn't
fly out. Sam comes up and takes the sweater from Nick, patting
it as though it were a wounded animal. Nick and Sam advance
slowly into the darkness.

                         HAROLD
               They make a weird little sound, like
               this --

He demonstrates the sound of a BAT CHITTER.

                         NICK
                    (dramatically)
               It's quiet here. Too quiet.

                         SAM
                    (picks up hairdryer as weapon)
               That's funny, my watch has stopped too.

Sam moves up next to them as they cautiously approach the spot.
Harold leans close to Sam's ear and makes the BAT CHITTER very
loud. Sam jumps.

                         SAM
               Shit!

The bat flys out past them and begins its frightened circuit of
the room again. All three guys are swiping at it. Harold goes
over to a window and opens it wide.

                         HAROLD
               Maybe it'll split.

As soon as the window is up two more bats fly in.

                         NICK
               Okay! Now we got a fair fight.

68 INT. DAUGHTER'S BEDROOM - NIGHT 68

Karen slips into the room and the ruckus up in the attic is
louder until she closes the door. She goes over to her bed
and sits down. She stares at the sleeping bulk that is her
husband, Richard.

69 EXT. SUMMER HOUSE - NIGHT   69

Very quiet. Middle of the night. There is the blue glow of
television in the den window.

70 INT. DEN - NIGHT   70

Nick is all alone in the den. He lies on a sofa with a liquor
glass balanced on his chest. He stares past it at the TV screen
where an old movie is playing. The volume is so low it's barely
audible.

Sam comes into the room, wearing only jeans. He leans over
the back of a chair, rubs his eyes, and watches the set a moment.
He nods toward the TV.

                         SAM
          What is that?

                         NICK
          I'm not sure.

                         SAM
          What's it about?

                         NICK
          I don't know.

                         SAM
          Who's that?

                         NICK
          I think the one in the hat did something
          terrible.

                         SAM
          Like what?

                         NICK
          You're so analytical. Sometimes you
          just have to let art flow over you.

                         SAM
          I'm hungry. I had a really dirty dream.

                         NICK
          Was it about Karen?

                         SAM
          Why do you say that?

                                                  CONTINUED:

CONTINUED:

                    NICK
          Why should anything have changed?

                    SAM
          You're the one she always wanted.

                    NICK
          In the old days I wasn't emotionally
          equipped to satisfy her. Now, the   *
          equipment doesn't work at all.   *

Sam winces, pained.

                    SAM
          Why are we talking about this? Come
          into the kitchen with me.

Sam stands up as Nick slowly begins to rouse himself.

                    SAM
          I think she found what she was looking
          for in Richard.

                    NICK
                    (after a beat)
          Yup.

They look at each other. And then they laugh. They walk
through the dining room toward the kitchen.

                    NICK
          Be careful what you want, young lady --

                    SAM AND NICK
                    (together)
          -- for you will surely get it.

71 INT. KITCHEN   71

Sam and Nick are laughing again as they push through the kitchen
door. They stop suddenly. Sitting at the far end of the kitchen
table is Richard. He has a beer, a sandwich and its makings
neatly arranged before him.

                    RICHARD
          Hi.

Sam and Nick exchange worried glances.

                    SAM
          Hey, Richard, what are you doing up?
          Why didn't you come in?

Sam goes to the refrigerator behind Richard.

                                                        CONTINUED:

CONTINUED: 71

> RICHARD
> I didn't realize anybody else was up.

Sam shoots a relieved look to Nick.

> RICHARD
> I've been thinking about your friend,
> Alex.

Nick nods, surprised.

> NICK
> Did you ever meet him?

> RICHARD
> No. Karen's told me some. I'm ima-
> gining mostly.

Sam brings a beer and some leftover reception food to the table.

> RICHARD
> I can never make it through the night.
> Insomnia. Karen doesn't even know it.

> NICK
> I might have something that could help
> you sleep.

> RICHARD
> (gives him a look)
> No thanks. I don't really mind it so
> much. Sometimes, with my boys and my
> wife upstairs asleep, I just sit down-
> stairs alone, and it's so ... quiet.
> I hate the fact that I can't sleep, but
> I don't mind the time alone. It's real
> thinking time. You don't get much of
> that at the office. It gives me a chance
> to remember what's important. Does that
> sound simple-minded?

Nick shakes his head.

> RICHARD
> Sometimes I think the thing about kids
> is they're instant priorities. You know
> you have to protect them and provide for
> them. Sometimes it means your life isn't
> exactly what you want it to be. There's
> some asshole at work you have to kow-tow
> to and sometimes you find yourself doing
> things you never thought you'd do. But
> you try to minimize that stuff and be
> the best person you can be.

CONTINUED:

CONTINUED: -37-

He takes a drink and studies their faces. He doesn't want to   71
seem foolish.

                         RICHARD
              But you set your priorities and that's
              the way life is. I wonder if your
              friend Alex knew that. One thing's
              for sure -- he couldn't live with it.

Nick stares at him. Sam too, his sandwich-making hands poised
and frozen in surprise.

                         RICHARD
              I know I shouldn't talk. You guys
              knew him. But the thing is, nobody
              said it was going to be fun. At
              least nobody said it to me.

A72 DISSOLVE TO SUNRISE - BRIDGE OVER THE BEAUFORT RIVER   A72

     A TITLE APPEARS: FRIDAY

72   EXT. MAINSTREET - MORNING   72

     Close on two sets of jogging feet: one is Harold's perfectly
     broken-in running shoes, the other Nick's battered, ripped
     tennis shoes. The men are jogging very slowly along the
     still empty Mainstreet. Harold is in his running gear,
     Nick in jeans and sweatshirt. Nick is struggling.

     They begin to walk. Harold looks at Nick's feet with concern.

                         HAROLD
              You can't run in those. I'll get you
              some shoes.

                                                                   *
                                                                   *

                         HAROLD

              I'm about to tell you something I'm
              not supposed to tell anyone.

                         NICK
              Then maybe you shouldn't.

                         HAROLD
              I already told Alex.

                                                        CONTINUED:

CONTINUED: -38-

                              NICK   72
              And look what happened to him.

                              HAROLD
                         (ignores him)
              In a few months a very large conglo-
              merate is going to buy my very small
              company. And anyone who has our stock
              is going to triple their money.

                              NICK
                         (impressed)
              Wow. So that's how Alex could afford
              to buy the land from you.

                              HAROLD
              That's right. Maybe you should use it
              to get into another line of work.

                              NICK
              You never learn do you?

                              HAROLD
                         (shakes his head)
              By telling you this, I have just violated
              about sixteen regulations of the Securities
              Exchange Commission. So please don't repeat   *
              it.

                              NICK
              Repeat what?

          Harold smiles. They walk on.

                              HAROLD
              I loved Alex.
                         (he looks at Nick)
              What happened between him and Sarah
              hurt, I can't deny it. But that was
              five years ago, and we all got over it.
              I think they felt as bad as I did.
              You know, they only slept together a
              few times, but, in a way, their love
              affair had been going on forever.

                              NICK
              She didn't marry Alex.

          Harold acknowledges the thought, nods at his friend.

       73 EXT. DRIVEWAY IN FRONT OF SUMMER HOUSE - MORNING   * 73

           LATER. A little group is out at Richard and Karen's rented car
           as Richard throws a suitcase in the back seat. Karen watches as
           Richard shakes hands and says goodbye to Harold, Sarah and Sam,

then waves again to Meg, who is up on the porch in her robe.   73
Richard turns to Karen and the others beat an uncomfortable
retreat as Richard pecks her cheek and gets in the car -- alone.
Karen watches him for a moment, then goes over and leans down
to speak to him at the driver's window. Neither of them looks
happy.

74   INT. KITCHEN - DAY   74

Sarah is alone in here. She stands before the open door of the
large refrigerator, staring at its contents. After a beat, she
writes something new on the shopping list that is stuck to the
freezer door. Again she returns to her frozen pose and stares
some more. Michael comes in, bleary-eyed and newly awake. He
moves up to Sarah and cautiously peeks around her into the
refrigerator. He glances between her and the open refrigerator,
mystified. Finally --

                         MICHAEL
               That's the trouble with these things,
               you have to watch them every minute.

She smiles. He takes the cream out of the refrigerator and goes
over to the coffee maker. He begins opening cabinet doors in
search of a cup.

                         MICHAEL
               Did I miss Karen and Richard?

                         SARAH
               Nope. Just Richard. Karen is staying
               the weekend.

                         MICHAEL
                    (eyebrows raised)
               But not Richard?

                         SARAH
               He went back to be with the kids.

                         MICHAEL
               Hmmmm. Interesting. How did Richard
               feel about that?

                         SARAH
               Michael, if you're going to sleep
               this late, you're gonna miss a few
               minidramas.

                         MICHAEL
               I just hope you'll wake me for any-
               thing really ugly.

Karen and Sam come down the porch steps and head for Harold's
Mercedes, which is parked beside a good-looking Jeep.

                    KAREN
          How do actors remember all those lines?

                    SAM
          Well, my wife used to help me, but now
          my maid does.

                    KAREN
          Your maid?

                    SAM
          Yeah. That's how she learned English.

Harold comes to the back door, sticks his head out and calls
to them.

                    HAROLD
          Sarah says to make three of those milks
          non-fat.
                    (they acknowledge)
          You're sure you don't mind this?

                    KAREN
                    (looking at Sam)
          I won't remember that... will you be
          able to remember that?

Sam and Karen get into the Mercedes like smiling daters.

                    SAM
          You know, if we had gotten married, we'd
          be doing this together.

                    KAREN
          No, if we had gotten married, I'd be doing
          this myself.

Harold watches them, thoughtful.

INT. MASTER BEDROOM - DAY

Sarah sits on the bed with the telephone cradled against her
ear; she is meticulously folding linen as she talks. Meg
comes in with some of Sarah's clothes which she has tried on.
Sarah does not notice her yet.

                    SARAH
                    (into phone)
          ... No, I did not say that, Molly.
          I said, we'll see ... I don't have
                    (MORE)

                         SARAH (CONT'D)
                      (into phone)
        to explain it to you, young lady ...
                      (Sarah notices Meg)
        ... I want you to do it because I
        said so! Do you hear me? ...

Sarah exchanges a self-conscious look with Meg as she listens
to Molly. She motions to Meg for a hit off Meg's cigarette.
When she speaks again her tone is softer.

                         SARAH
                      (into phone)
        ... All right, you can do that. Tell
        Carmelina I said it was okay. I love
        you, sweetheart. Daddy will call you
        later.

She hangs up. Meg holds up one of Sarah's dresses against
her body, modeling.

                         SARAH
        Sometimes I can't believe what I
        hear myself saying.

                         _____

75   INT. OFFICE - DAY   75

Nick is moving slowly along the book shelves, scanning titles
on rows of video cassettes. Suddenly he finds himself face to
face with something else entirely: there on the shelves is a
complete, almost-new video camera and recording rig. His face
lights up.

77   INT. LIVING ROOM - DAY   77

Nick has set up the video camera and equipment in the living
room and we start CLOSE ON his image in the VIDEO MONITOR on
the camera. He is sitting on the couch trying to interview
himself. His voice and posture shift subtly between his
"Interviewer" persona and his "Guest" persona. The effect is
a touch schizophrenic. As he talks, we slowly move out from
behind the video camera to see him directly on the couch. The
"Guest" is evasive, not too enthusiastic about this.

                         NICK
                      (Interviewer)
        ... So you came back from Vietnam a
        "changed man".
                      (Guest)
        Well, why don't you just tell everybody.
                      (Interviewer)
        And then in 1972 you returned to the
        University of Michigan to enter the
        doctoral program in psychology. But
        you just couldn't seem to finish that
        dissertation.
                      (Guest)
        I could have. I chose not to. I'm not
        hung up on this completion thing.
                      (Interviewer)
        Then it was on to a series of jobs, all
        of which you quit.
                      (MORE)

                        NICK (CONT'D)   -42-   77
                  (Guest)
What are you getting at? I was evolving.
I'm <u>still</u> evolving.
                  (Interviewer)
But your real fame came as a radio
psychologist on KCBS in San Francisco.   *

Chloe watches unseen from the shadows of the den.

                        NICK
                  (Guest)
I wouldn't call it "fame". I had a
small, deeply disturbed following.
Are we almost done here?
                  (Interviewer)
What are you doing now -- or I should
say, what have you evolved into now?
                  (Guest)
Oh ... I'm in sales.
                  (Interviewer)
What are you selling?
                  (Guest, mumbles)
I don't have to answer that.
                  (looks off camera, as if to lawyer)
Do I have to answer that?

Harold sticks his head in the living room.

                        HAROLD
Nick, we're leaving now. Have you seen
Chloe?

                        NICK
                  (as Interviewer, perturbed)
Harold, we're on the air here.
                  (as Guest)
Hey, sorry, I gotta go.
                  (as Interviewer)
Just answer that last question!
                  (as Guest, grabs his own shirt, roughly)
Listen, pal, I <u>said</u> I've got to go!

He pushes himself against the back of the sofa.

EXT.   CAROLINA CAOUNTRYSIDE - ROAD (VARIOUS SHOTS) - DAY

The jeep zips through heavily-wooded, autumn-hued country
to the beat of the sixties ROCK 'N ROLL playing on its tape
deck.

INT.   JEEP - DAY

Michael sits next to the driving Harold. Nick and Chloe are
in back. Nick is entranced by the passing scenery.

                    HAROLD
          ... So what happened to your partner?

                    MICHAEL
          He wasn't my partner. He just had the
          original idea for the club. He's out
          of it now. We weren't conducive. We'd
          get together and hyper each other into
          a frenzy. Then his wife left him for a
          younger woman. He couldn't make love.
          Eventually he was hospitalized for being
          such a nerd.

                    HAROLD
                 (trying to follow this)
          So he's out of it?

                    MICHAEL
          He's out. It's just me, looking for
          investors.

                    CHLOE
          Alex and I made love the night before
          he died. It was fantastic.

                                        CONTINUED:

The others aren't sure what prompted this.   80

                          NICK
                       (finally)
          He went out with a bang, not a whimper.

81   INT. KITCHEN (THE SUMMER HOUSE) - DAY   81

Sarah and Meg are in the early stages of preparing what will
be an enormous meal centered around a stuffed turkey. Sarah's
Cuisinart is doing heavy duty. Meg is messing with what appears
to be dough for a pie, but her mind is roaring in another direction --

                          MEG
          ... If they're not married, they're
          gay. If they're not gay, they've
          just broken up with the most wonder-   *
          ful woman in the world or they've   *
          just broken up with a bitch who looked
          just like me. They're in transition
          from a monogamous relationship and
          they need more "space". Or they're
          tired of "space", but they just can't
          commit. They want to commit, but
          they're afraid to get close. They
          want to get close, but you don't want
          to get near them.

                          SARAH
                       (laughs)
          It can't be that bad.

                          MEG
          I'm going easy. You don't know. I've
          been out there dating for twenty years.
          I've gotten so I can tell in fifteen
          seconds if there's a chance in the world.

                          SARAH
          Well, at least you're giving them a
          fair shot.

                          MEG
          That's easy for you to say, married to
          Harold, "The Perfect Man"...

Something flits across Sarah's face here, but Meg either misses
it or chooses to ignore it.

                          MEG   *
          Sometimes, I think I don't even want a   *
          man anymore.   *
                       (a beat)
                        (MORE)

MEG (CONT'D)
So here I sit on my ticking biological
clock, and the only thing I've known
in my whole life is that I want to have
a child.

Sarah gives her a sudden look. They share a strong memory of
a traumatic moment from their history. Meg responds to it --

MEG
Don't remind me. It probably was the
right thing to do at the time, but ...

SARAH
So what do you do?

Meg is slow to answer. She rolls her dough.

MEG
I'm going to have a baby.

82   INT. SUPERMARKET - DAY   82

Karen and Sam each push a shopping cart, one completely full,
the other filling. They are passing the freezer cases.

SAM
... I don't see her as much as I'd
like. She was very young when Robin
and I were divorced. Now she's got a
new father. Sometimes I think it's
just confusing to her when I'm around.
I don't know.

Karen nods her understanding. They have reached the ice cream
display. Sam looks down at the ice cream with her. They are
tempted. They pantomime resistance.

SAM
I don't need it.

KAREN
God knows I don't.

They move a fraction of an inch away from the ice cream, but
stop.

SAM
Maybe we should think of the others.

KAREN
We don't want to be selfish.

CONTINUED:

CONTINUED: -46-

                          SAM
                     (reaching deep)
          I know Sarah and Meg would probably
          want this double chocolate chip.

                         KAREN
          They have no self-control.

They laugh as they load up the cart and move on.

                          SAM
          I don't know. Maybe I just don't
          want to give her the time. Could I
          be that big an asshole?

85 EXT. MEADOW AND WOODS (ON HAROLD'S LAND) - DAY   85

     Michael finishes taking a leak. Harold stands nearby, a stick
     in his hand.

                        MICHAEL
                     (exuberant)
          That's what's great about the outdoors,
          it's one giant toilet.

                         HAROLD
          Maybe you should put a spot like this
          in your club.

They walk on.

                        MICHAEL
          This thing is going to be big, Harold.
          You should take it more seriously.
          You'd have your own table waiting at
          all times.

                         HAROLD
          I'm considering the investment. I've
          always wanted my own table. Would I
          have a chair, too?

                        MICHAEL
          Remember senior year we were all going
          to get together and buy that land near
          Saginaw. What happened with that?

                         HAROLD
          None of us had any money.

                        MICHAEL
          Oh, yeah.
                     (a beat)
          That's when property was a crime.

Sarah sits staring at Meg, her expression slightly dazed. Meg

works busily away, cutting apples for her pie.   84

                    MEG
          You're a doctor. Doctors know every-
          thing. So just be supportive for a
          minute and shut up.
                    (Sarah nods)
          I've been taking my temperature and
          I know I'm ovulating right now. The
          ground is ready. I just need some-
          one to plant the seed.

                    SARAH
          Yeah, but who's going to be the
          lucky farmer?

                    MEG
          These are the best guys I know, my
          favorite men in the world. Unfortunately
          Nick, as I discover I'm the last to know,
          is no longer a candidate. Michael is
          a possibility but -- considering
          everything -- a fallback position.

                    SARAH
          ... So to speak.

                    MEG
          That leaves Sam.

                    SARAH
          Oh, Harold's not good enough for you?

                    MEG
          I'd love it, but I wouldn't ask that
          of you. Harold's got enough kids.

                    SARAH
          That's very considerate. Too bad
          Richard left.

Meg just smiles.

                    SARAH
          Have you discussed this with Sam or
          are you planning a surprise party?

                    MEG
          Why should he have a problem with it?
          There will be no obligations. I love
          him, as a friend. I assume he loves
          me. He'd do anything for me.

Sarah shakes her head as if to clear it.

CONTINUED:

                              SARAH
              Somehow I feel it isn't quite this
              simple.. For one thing, you know,
              it doesn't always happen the first
              time.

                              MEG
              That's not what they told us in
              high school.

83   INT.   DILAPIDATED FARM HOUSE (ON HAROLD'S LAND) - DAY

      Chloe stands in the center of the wrecked central room of the
      ancient farm house. There is a chaos of mess about: wood,
      tools, a sawhorse, discarded debris. Alex was refurbishing it
      with Chloe's help and it has the look of slow, small-scale
      renovation. On the floor in one corner is a mattress where
      they obviously took their breaks.

      Nick stands at one of the large holes which were once windows,
      staring out. Now he turns, with a vigor and glee that we
      have not seen before, and strides to a similar hole on the
      other side of the house.

                              NICK
                This is great! This is really great!

      He stands at the other hole looking out. As Chloe moves up
      behind him, we go with her and get our first view of the land.
      Beyond the ragged meadow are thick, rolling woods, dark and lush.
      Michael and Harold are out there in the distance.

                              CHLOE
              Alex loved this place.

                              NICK
              I can understand it. It's great!

                              CHLOE
                          (looking at him)
              You remind me of Alex.

      Nick does a big take and eyes her queerly.

                              NICK
              I ain't him.

TV SCREEN. A videotaped interview with Michael which
Nick has recorded in the living room is playing on the
big Sony in the den. Eventually we will see that the
viewers include Nick, Michael, Chloe and Sam. But now
we see only Michael and Sam on tape.

                    MICHAEL (ON TAPE)
          ...nobody thinks they're an asshole.
          Nobody thinks they're a bad person. I'm
          not even claiming that people always
          think they're doing the right thing.
          They may know that they're doing some-
          thing dishonest or insensitive or mani-
          pulative. But they almost always think
          there's a good reason for doing it. They
          almost always think that it'll turn out
          for the best in the end. Even if it's
          just that it turns out best for them. By
          definition, what is best for them is what's
          best. In addition, you instantly come up
          against a question of style. My style
          may be too direct. Perhaps, given my style,
          I seem more nakedly opportunistic or jerky
          or what was the other thing?

                    SAM (ON TAPE)
          Manipulative?

                    MICHAEL (ON TAPE)
          Whatever. But really all that's happening
          is that I'm trying to get what I want.
          Which is what everybody does. It's
          just that some of their styles are so
          warm or charming or sincere or otherwise
          phoney that you don't realize they're
          just trying to get what they want. So you
          see my transparent efforts are in a way much
          more honest and admirable.

                    SAM (ON TAPE)
          Why is it that what you just said sounds
          like a massive rationalization?

                    MICHAEL (ON TAPE)
          Don't knock rationalization. Where
          would we be without it? I don't know
          a soul who could get through the day with-
          out two or three juicy rationalizations.
          They're more important than sex.

                    SAM (ON TAPE)
          Oh, come on. Nothing's more important
          than sex.

                    MICHAEL (ON TAPE)
          Oh yeah? Have you ever gone a week with-
          out a rationalization?

89   INT. KITCHEN - NIGHT   89

The place is crowded, everybody fussing and fretting over
various pots. Finished food is piling up on the counters,
wine bottles are opened, gravy poured. Karen ladles Motown
Mogumbo into various bowls. Harold is making notations on
a small pad. Sam turns from a dramatically finished sauce
to his newly drained pasta and hurls strands of it at the
refrigerator, where there are previously-tested remnants.
Sarah eyes this ancient test with bemused irritation.

                    SAM
               (reacts to Sarah's look)
          It's still the best way to determine
          if it's ready.

                    HAROLD
               (to Meg, as she enters)
          What's your shoe size?

                    MEG
          Seven. I used to be a six and a half.

                    HAROLD
               (he notes it)
          Your feet grow as they get old.

                    MICHAEL
          I wish everything did.

CONTINUED:

Sarah scans the room, satisfied with what she sees, and focuses 89
on Sam who is once again touching up the sauce.

                    SARAH
          Sam, how much longer? Everything
          is going to get cold.

                    MEG
               (looking over Sam's shoulder)
          Oh no. In twelve years, you haven't
          learned to make anything else?

                    SAM   *
          I've improved it.   *

                    MEG   *
          Now it's edible.   *

                    SARAH
          The meal is starting. Everybody grab
          something and get out of my kitchen.

Karen and Sarah, each with two bowls of Mogumbo, start the
parade into the dining room.

90   INT.   DINING ROOM - NIGHT   90

As the crowd moves into the dining room, we hear the first bars
of the brassy THEME TO SAM'S SHOW blasting from the adjacent
den. Sam, cradling his creation, winces as he hears the tune.

                    NICK (O.S.)
          Oh-oh. Here he is -- J. T. Lancer!
          Take a look at that hunk of man, kids.

                    SAM
          Turn that off!

He quickly deposits the pasta on the table and heads toward the
offending TV.

91   INT.   DEN - NIGHT   91

Too late. The group has shifted into the den to see the
opening credits of his show. Harold gently restrains Sam,
until it's too late.

                    SAM
          Why are you doing this to me?

We see the opening credits of "J. T. LANCER". Sam is a private
eye in New Orleans, a fact clearly demonstrated in the title
montage. There he is: leaping into a Ferrarri; leaping off a
Basin Street balcony; leaping across the bar in a strip joint;

and leaping into bed with a bevy of bayou babes. The se-   91
quence ends with a sly signature thumbs-up and wink from the
tough shamus. This last draws ecstatic hoots. Meg faints
into Sam's arms. Sarah thumbs-up and winks at Sam --

                    SARAH
          Say, baby, let's eat.

They head into the dining room.

                    SAM
                 (grumbling)
          The pasta's ruined now.

                    MICHAEL.
                 (to Sam)
          Do you get money every time that
          comes on?

                    SAM
          Yeah.

93   INT. DINING ROOM   93

LATER. The meal has been severely dented. Much wine has been
consumed. They're feeling the effects. Michael is whispering
in an intimate manner to Chloe, who giggles. Nick and Harold
both have noted this. They exchange looks.

                         MEG
                    (to Sam)
          ... What am I hearing? I don't want
          to hear that.

                         SAM
          What d'ya mean?

                         MEG
          Video games? You're telling me you
          relax with video games?

                         MICHAEL
          Don't knock video games.

                         MEG
          Jesus, I let you guys out of my sight
          for a little while and you develop a
          bunch of moronic interests.

                         HAROLD
          Don't knock morons.

                                          CONTINUED:

                         SAM
                    (to Meg)
          Would you prefer I got into heavy
          drugs?
                    (a beat)
          No offense, Nick.

Nick waves it off, no offense taken.

                         KAREN
          Sarah?

Down at the end of the table, Sarah is crying. Karen, who's
sitting next to her, now has a comforting hand on her. Sarah,
embarrassed, wipes her eyes with her napkin. She immediately
tries to regain her composure.

                         SARAH
          He should be here.
                    (a weird laugh)
          I feel like we should've had a
          chair for Alex.

There is a moment of silence, pregnant. Then Sarah snuffles
again, and smiles.

                         SARAH
          Of course, we don't have enough food.

She smiles. They all want to comfort her; they reassure her
with their looks. She starts to cry again.

                         SARAH
          It's just so familiar, this ...
                    (she vaguely indicates the table
                     and group)
          ... and I love you all so much. I
          know that sounds gross, doesn't it?

                         KAREN
          No, it doesn't.

                         SARAH
                    (getting control again)
          I feel like I was at my best when I was
          with you people.

                         HAROLD   *
          I like you now.   *

                         SAM
          I know what Sarah means. When I lost   *
          touch with this group, I lost my idea
          of what I should be.
                    (a beat)
                         (MORE)

SAM (CONT'D)
Maybe that's what happened to Alex.
At least we expected something of
(MORE)

                          SAM (CONT'D)
          each other. I think we needed that.

Again there is a long pause. Harold reaches out to touch Meg's
nape affectionately.

                          HAROLD
          Not me. Getting away from you people
          was the best thing that ever happened
          to me. How much sex, fun, and friend-
          ship can one man take? ... I had to
          get out in the world and get dirty.

                          KAREN   *
          Half the stuff I did, I did to piss   *
          off my parents. And it worked.   *

Michael is not willing to let this moment escape just yet. His
tone is sincere, subdued --

                          MICHAEL   *
          No, I think Sam's right. There was some-
          thing in me then that made me want to
          go to Harlem and teach those ghetto kids.

                          MEG
                    (nods at that)
          And I was going to go help ...
                    (slight embarrassment)
          ... "the scum", as I so compassionately
          refer to them now.

                          HAROLD
                    (resisting the tide)
          Some of them were scum.

                          MICHAEL
          Some of us are scum.

                          HAROLD
          So what's the thrust here? We were
          great then and we're shit now? I
          don't like where this is going.

Harold looks toward Nick for support. But Nick seems to be
concentrating on his plate. He doesn't look up.

                          SARAH
          No, we're not saying that. You know
          that, Harold. I'm sure we all think
          there's a lot of good left in us. I
          don't know, I just hate to think that
          it was all just -- fashion.
                          HAROLD
          What?
                          SARAH
          Our commitment.

                                              CONTINUED:

CONTINUED: -57-

                          SAM
        It wasn't. We accomplished things.

                        HAROLD
        ... all evidence to the contrary.

                        SARAH
                   (to Harold, irritated)
        Now you're just taking a position.

                          MEG
        Sometimes I think I put that time down,
        pretend it wasn't real, just so I can
        live with how I am now.
                   (to Harold)
        Do you know what I mean?

                        HAROLD
        Nick, help me with these bleeding
        hearts.

                         NICK
                   (after a pause)
        I know what Alex would say.

                        SARAH
        What?

                         NICK
        What's for dessert?

Chloe giggles. Sarah frowns, as does Meg who shakes her head.
Nick addresses Meg, in mock defense.

                         NICK
        I'm not cynical about dessert.

94 INT. KITCHEN - NIGHT   94

    Sarah, Meg and Sam come in with the cleared dessert dishes.
    They are stopped cold by the sight of the cleaning-up job
    ahead. In that moment, the first rhythmic bars of "Ain't
    Too Proud To Beg" by The Temptations blast from the speakers
    in the wall.

94A INT. DEN   94A*

    Harold, who has put the record on the stereo, kisses the image
    of The Temptations on the album jacket, puts it down, and boogies
    back toward the dining room.

95 INT. KITCHEN/DINING ROOM - THE CLEANING-UP MONTAGE   95
          (VARIOUS SHOTS)

    The group clears, cleans, washes and wraps to the beat of the
    song. Some of them are lip-synching to the song, others deli-

                                              CONTINUED:

vering dishes from room to sink with Motown-style choreography.   95
Harold engages Karen in an impromptu two-step near the disposal,
Meg loads the dishwasher like a Supreme. In the midst of this,
we find --

96 INT. DINING ROOM - NIGHT   -59-   96

Harold, Michael and Sam in the dining room. Michael is taking
away the last empty coffee cups as Sam collects and shakes the
napkins and Harold carefully folds the tablecloth around its
crumbs.

                    SAM
               (to Harold, mid-conversation)
          ... I think I've been slow to realize
          that people our own age, with histories
          just like ours -- having gone through
          all that same stuff -- can be dishonest,
          unprincipled, backstabbing ... sleazeballs.

                    MICHAEL
               (arms loaded)
          I could've told you that a long time
          ago.

Michael goes out to the kitchen.

                    SAM
          I was prejudiced in their favor.   *
          Just because they look like us, and   *
          talk like us, I thought they were   *
          going to think like us. I've been   *
          real stupid about that sometimes,   *
          and have gotten sucked in.   *

                    HAROLD
          I think Alex felt that same thing
          very strongly.

                    SAM
          Alex was always very forgiving.

                    HAROLD
          Well, not so much lately. You didn't
          see him too much lately. He was
          pretty disgusted by what he was seeing
          around. He'd get angry.

                    SAM
          I never saw that.

                    HAROLD
          He was very forgiving of you.

The cleaning-up is complete and "Ain't Too Proud To Beg" has faded with the hub-bub. There's SLOW MUSIC here in the living room. Michael and Chloe are on the floor, talking intimately. Karen, Harold, Nick and Sarah are on the couch, passing a joint.

                    KAREN
      ...I know Richard will always be
      faithful to me.

                    HAROLD
      That's nice. A little trust.

                    KAREN
            (shakes her head, "no")
      Fear of herpes.

Harold and Nick sit side by side on the sofa. They're looking across the room at Michael, who is sitting very close to Chloe, murmuring to her.

                    NICK
      It's not right.

                    HAROLD
      Ummm. Alex is still warm. You
      can't blame Chloe, she's just a
      kid.

                    NICK
      Michael hasn't changed.

                    HAROLD
      Have you ever met Michael's girlfriend,
      Annie?
            (Nick shakes his head "no")
      She's incredible. She teaches the fourth
      grade.
            (a beat)
      She still teaches in Harlem.

Harold and Nick exchange a look and an ironic smile. They look back at Michael.

                    NICK
      It's not right.

Sarah plops down next to Nick with exaggerated exhaustion and puts her head on his shoulder.

                    SARAH
      I can't keep my eyes open. I don't
      want to go to bed, but I think I'm
      going to have to.

                                    CONTINUED:

                          NICK
          You really don't want to?

                          SARAH
                     (yawning "no")
          But I've got to.

                          NICK
          But you don't want to?
                     (a questioning look from Sarah)
          Come with me.

He helps her up.

INT. MAID'S ROOM - NIGHT

Meg is sitting with her back against the headboard, hugging
her knees. Sam sits sideways on the bed before her. He is
a man in shock, trying to get his head around it. Finally --

                          SAM
          What? You want me to do what?

                                             CONTINUED:

                              MEG
              Come on, Sam, don't make me say it
              again.

                              SAM
              Meg, you're giving me a massive
              headache.

                              MEG
              You're not gonna use that old
              excuse are you?

He sits there in silence a long moment.

                              MEG
              You have good genes.

Reflexively, he looks down at his beautifully faded and pressed
Levis. One of his hands moves involuntarily toward his fly,
protectively.

100   INT. DEN - NIGHT   100

Michael is alone on the couch, cheerfully rolling a joint on
the coffee table. Nick sits down beside him.

                              NICK
              Where'd Chloe go?

Michael looks up, barely able to hide his maniacally pleased
expression.

                              MICHAEL
              She's coming right back.

Nick nods. He digs in his pocket and comes out with the small
white disc of a Quaalude. He holds it in his palm and regards
it reflectively.

                              NICK
                        (finally)
              Nah. I'm not in the mood.

Nick starts to put it away, but Michael stops him.

                              MICHAEL
              What is that, a lude?

                              NICK
                        (innocently)
              You want it?

Michael does. Nick gives it to him.

                              MICHAEL
              What do you think -- a half?

                          NICK   100
                       (considers)
         Full stomach ... I'd take a whole.

                        MICHAEL
         Yes, I'm sure you would.
                       (picks up his glass)
         What the hell. L'Chayim!

He downs the whole tablet.

102 INT. MAID'S ROOM - NIGHT   102

Now both Meg and Sam lean against the headboard. They are fully
clothed and Sam has his arm around her. He speaks quietly,
tenderly.

                          SAM
              ... When it's born, it's just the
              most amazing thing. Your whole
              life changes, forever. There's a
              little shift in your perceptions
              of the world and forever you're
              responsible for another living
              thing. It's wonderful. But it's
              a huge commitment, a commitment
              that has nothing to do with legal
              obligations or legal names ...
              I'm sorry. I would love to help
              you, but I can't.

                                                            CONTINUED:

Meg is quiet for a while.

               MEG
    You know, you're really something.
    I love you.

               SAM
       (misunderstands)
    Meg, I can't, really --

               MEG
       (stopping him)
    No, no, I accept that. I just mean
    I really love you. You're a nice
    person.

               SAM
       (looks at her)
    Yeah? Really?

She nods. Hugs him tighter. He smiles.

               SAM
    So, you wanna fuck?
       (she laughs)
    Just kidding!

103 INT. DEN - NIGHT   10-3

Nick sits at one end of the sofa, Chloe close beside him. At
the other end, beside her, Michael is sprawled, out cold, dead
to the world. The glow of the TV lights their faces, and, in
fact, Nick is sort of watching, but the sound is off. What we
hear is soft, midnight ROCK 'N ROLL. Nick reaches across Chloe
to extract a half-full wine glass from Michael's grip.

               NICK
    ... Then, one day I was driving home
    and they were running a tape of one
    of my shows. And I heard myself
    talking to someone who had called up,
    someone in real pain. And I had
    listened to them for forty-five
    seconds, and I'm acting as though I
    know them and understand and have some-
    thing useful to say about their life.
    And the worst part was, they believed
    me.
       (a beat)
    I quit the next day.

They are silent for a few moments.

               CHLOE
    You helped me.

CONTINUED:

It takes a moment for this to penetrate Nick's foggy mind. When
it does, he grimaces, and looks at her.

                    CHLOE
          I was fifteen. My family was living
          in Oakland. I used to listen to you
          every night. One night I called you
          up. I was real upset -- I thought there
          was something wrong with me. I thought
          I was some kind of pervert.

                    NICK
          What'd I say?

                    CHLOE
          You said it was okay.
                    (a beat)
          As long as I did my homework and went
          to bed at a reasonable hour.

Nick winces.

                    CHLOE
          You were right. It was okay. And
          it helped.

Nick looks at her and accepts that.

104 INT. MASTER BEDROOM - NIGHT   104

Harold lies on his side of the bed, eyes closed. Sarah is
sitting up in bed, legs in lotus position, facing him, her
hands working incessantly at the silky border of their blanket,
repeatedly gathering it into bunches in her palms. As she
does this, the blanket is slowly pulled off of Harold. She
is wide awake.

                    HAROLD
          I don't want to discuss this now.

                    SARAH
          Why, you have some more people you
          want to tell about the stock thing?

                    HAROLD
          This is really a lovely side of you.
          Remind me to get some more cocaine in
          the morning.

                    SARAH
          That is not it, Harold. If you go
          around telling everyone about this
          stock deal, it's going to blow up
          in your face. Who are you going
          to tell next, Michael? He came down
          here to find investors for that moronic
                    (MORE)

club, didn't he?

                    HAROLD
        He came down here for Alex's funeral.

                    SARAH
        Maybe.

                    HAROLD
                (reacts to this)
        Whoa! You're in no condition to discuss
        this.

                    SARAH
        Harold, you can't change people's
        lives for them. Who are you, John
        Bairsford Tipton?

                    HAROLD
        I'm going to sleep.

                    SARAH
        How can you sleep? I'm not even tired.

105   INT. DEN - NIGHT   105

        Chloe sleeps on Nick's lap. Michael has not moved. Nick stares
        at the blinking television. The MUSIC fades away.

        DISSOLVE TO pounding surf. Rising sun.

        A TITLE APPEARS: SATURDAY

106   EXT. BEACHFRONT - MORNING   106

        This morning, Sam has joined Harold and Nick for a run along the
        beachfront. They are slowing to a walk now; Sam is only slightly
        less bushed than Nick. Harold is not even sweating.

                    SAM
        ... Some people think suicide is the
        ultimate act of self-absorption.

                    NICK
        Why do you bring that up? Alex didn't
        commit suicide. It was an accident.

                    HAROLD
        That's right. He was shaving. Alex
        always had hairy wrists. I always
        thought masturbation was the ultimate
        act of self-absorption.

                    SAM
        Do you jerk off?

                                          CONTINUED:

                         HAROLD
          Does a bear have fleas?

                          SAM
                      (corrects him)
          No -- Does a bear shit in the woods?

                         HAROLD
          Does a bear jerk off?

                          NICK
          I shit in the woods, but I can't jerk
          off.

                          SAM
          Do you think we're all trying to avoid
          dealing with Alex? Every time it comes
          up, somebody changes the subject.

                          NICK
          Hey, it's a dead subject.

Sam shoots him a look.

                          SAM
          I'm getting tired of all these jokes.
          What are we afraid of? To show our
          feelings? Or are we mad at him for
          leaving us here with no explanations?

                          NICK
          I could say something really funny
          about that, but I won't.

Sam doesn't think that's funny. Harold notices something up
ahead.

                         HAROLD
          Great, they got here early.

He takes off running toward the Summer House; where a van is
parked in the driveway.

107   EXT. DRIVEWAY - MORNING   107

Sam and Nick, having straggled in, walk up to the neatly-printed,
beige and green van in the driveway. On the side of the van is
the large silhouette of a dog running in jogging shoes. In large
letters underneath is painted -- RUNNING DOG ATHLETIC FOOTWEAR
CENTERS. And under that, in smaller type, the twenty-six South-
eastern locations. To the side, the motto: "Sole Food for
Every Sport".

Harold comes back out of the house with a fifty year-old DRIVER,
who wears a beige and green Running Dog uniform. Harold stops

                                                      CONTINUED:

on the verandah as the Driver heads back to the van.   107

                    HAROLD
          Thanks a lot, Tony. I appreciate it.

                    DRIVER
          Yes sir, Mr. Cooper. My pleasure.
          Have a nice weekend now.

The Driver gets in, waves and drives off. Sam and Nick watch
him go. They're impressed.

                    SAM
                (to Harold)
          Yes sir, Mr. Cooper.

110 INT. KITCHEN - DAY   110

     Meg comes in. She is so intent on her first cup of coffee from
     the steaming coffee maker that she at first misses the sight
     on the kitchen table. With a mug and ashtray safely in hand,
     she turns to the table. Neatly stacked at one end is a pyramid
     of shoe boxes from various athletic manufacturers. In bold
     letters on each box has been markered a name. She extracts
     the one marked "MEG" from the stack and sits down. She sips
     some coffee, lights a cigarette and opens her box, lifting out
     a bright, orange and green running shoe. She places it care-
     fully next to her ashtray and looks at it as if she's never
     seen anything like it before.

     We are in a FULL·SHOT of the kitchen now, in the soft morning
     light, and the CAMERA will now be LOCKED DOWN in this spot for
     the next three scenes. We DISSOLVE TO:

111 INT. KITCHEN - DAY   111

     A LITTLE LATER. Meg is still sitting in the same spot and is
     now reading the newspaper. Karen, in a robe, is busy and
     efficient at the stove, cooking up a storm. Nick sits at the
     table and is putting on his new pair of running shoes, a

                                               CONTINUED:

dazzling silver and blue. Karen brings a plate of food to   111
Meg and, as she does, we see that she is already wearing
her new shoes; they are bright yellow and orange. Meg nods
a "thank you".

                         KAREN
          So you just fell asleep?

                         MEG
                  (mock remembering)
          I said that, didn't I? Didn't I
          say that?

                         NICK
          About five times.

                         MEG
          I did not "know him" in the Biblical
          sense. Does that make it clear enough,
          Karen?

                         KAREN
          I don't know why you're so touchy.

                         MEG
          I don't know why you're so curious.

Nick has stood up and walked around. He looks at his feet
with pleasure.

                         NICK
          These feel great. I'm never taking
          these off. I'm going to sleep in them.

                         MEG
                  (looking up from paper, to Karen)
          That doesn't mean he's going to have
          sex with them.

                                              DISSOLVE TO:

112 INT. KITCHEN - DAY (CAMERA LOCKED OFF)   112

A LITTLE LATER. Meg and Nick are gone. Karen still cooks.
Sam and Chloe are at the table. Harold works at a counter.
The pyramid of shoe boxes is disappearing; the boxes are
scattered about the room. The two men are freshly showered.

                         HAROLD
                  (to Sam)
          So what do you think about Michael's
          latest brainstorm?

CONTINUED:

                              SAM   112
            I'm not sure I want to be part owner
            of some jet set greasy spoon. You
            think we could stall him for a while?

Karen has proudly brought a picture perfect breakfast plate
to Sam. They hear the ROAR of an engine from just outside
the window. It moves away.

                              SAM
            Jesus, what's that?

                            HAROLD
            Nick wanted to run out to the property
            again and be back before the game starts.

Chloe looks up, interested.   *

                                                        DISSOVE TO:

113   INT. KITCHEN - DAY (CAMERA LOCKED OFF)   113

A LITTLE LATER. Sarah is alone in here, huddled over a cup
of coffee, looking beat. Michael lurches into the doorway,
squints around and stumbles over to the coffee. He looks
worse than Sarah. He brings a cup to the table and sits down,
in pain. He notices the lone remaining shoe box, but it's
too far away to investigate.

                            MICHAEL
            Are we the first ones up?

114   EXT. DOCK - MORNING   114

Sam and Karen are out at the end of the long dock into the   *
river. They lean toward each other either for warmth or for   *
increased intimacy.

                              SAM
            Christ, who even knows what it was all
            about. You remember Alex used to call
            me Sam the Sham.

                            KAREN
            No, don't say that. It was real. I
            remember standing on campus with thou-
            sands of people listening to you. And
            you really moved them.

                              SAM
                        (shakes his head)
            But now ... I'm reaching millions of
            people every week and, hell, you know,
            it's just garbage.

                                                        CONTINUED:

                         KAREN   114
That's not true. You're entertaining
people. God knows we need that now.

                         SAM
Yeah? I don't know. I try. At least
once every show I try to put something
of value in there. But, I don't know...

                         KAREN
You do. I can see it. I feel like my
kids have gotten something out of J. T.
Lancer.

                              SAM
        Really?
                    (Karen reassures him)
        Kids. Well there you are. You've done
        something there. You've really built
        something with Richard, I'll bet.

Karen looks away a moment. When she speaks, there's no harshness
in her voice.

                              KAREN
        You know the secret of Richard? You
        remember my father?

Sam does, with disgust. What a jerk.

                              KAREN
        Well I didn't want that to happen to
        me. Richard looked like everything
        that had been missing in my childhood.
        I knew a guy like that could build a
        stable environment for children. And
        he did.
                    (she pauses)
        It's just that now, well ...

                              SAM
        What?

                              KAREN
        Well, you know. It's well, it's not
        like talking to you.
                    (Sam looks away, embarrassed and
                     pleased)
        All my life, deep inside, I felt there
        was something I wanted to express. I
        have always felt, I don't know ... stymied.
                    (she looks up)
        But, look, I'm proud of what I did. I'm
        doing a good job raising my sons. And
        if it meant I had to give up my writing,
        well, that's the way it goes!

Sam tries desperately to remember her writing. Karen sees his
struggle.

                              KAREN
        Oh, you probably don't even remember
        my writing.

                              SAM
        Sure I do.

                              KAREN
        It was just some poems and short stories.
                    (MORE)

                          KAREN (CONT'D)
          I didn't show them to many people.
                    (touches his knee)
          But what's the point of talking about
          it. I made my decision. My kids come
          first. It's just that now it leaves
          kind of, I don't know, a space. And
          all of Richard's country clubs and home
          improvements and business dinners,
          well ... it's pretty superficial stuff.

Sam, following as best he can, nods sympathetically.

                          KAREN
          I'm not complaining. Maybe I am.
          I'm sorry. Being with you opens
          me up somehow. Forgive me.

Sam puts a hand on her. No forgiveness necessary.

115 EXT. DILAPIDATED FARM HOUSE (ON HAROLD'S LAND) - DAY   115

Nick sits in a doorway of the old house looking off at the woods.

116 INT. SECOND FLOOR HALLWAY (THE SUMMER HOUSE) - DAY   116

Sarah is coming down the hall with an armload of linen as Karen
comes upstairs. From below Karen we HEAR the unmistakable
strains of the University of Michigan FIGHT SONG, "Hail to the
Victors" emanating from a television turned unreasonably loud.
Downstairs, Michael is singing the words, badly, along with
the music. There is a rumbling on the steps behind Karen, and
Harold, a football tucked snugly under his arm, tears up the
stairs past her and heads for his bedroom.

                          HAROLD
          I'm late, I'm late, for a very
          important date ...

He disappears into the bedroom as Sarah shares a familiar look
with Karen. Almost immediately, Harold reappears, wearing a
blue and gold Michigan Tam O' Shanter and muffler and heads back
downstairs.

                          HAROLD
                    (over his shoulder)
          Come on, girls, the game is starting.
          You don't want to miss any of the Blue.

He is gone. The women head for their respective rooms.

                          KAREN
          Time to wash my hair.

                          SARAH
          Me, I always read.

They go in and close their doors.

Starting at floor level, we see several sets of flashily-
bedecked, running shoe feet scattered among the rearranged
furniture. The game commentary blasts from the television
along with the crowd roar. The watchers, who we see in a
moment, are hurling their own abuse back at the tube, displeased
with the quality of everything they're seeing, from the play-
by-play to the coaching to the color of the opposition's uniforms.
There is a WHISTLE in the game and Sam's feet leap into the
air in protest. The camera rises to take in the action in the
den: Harold and Sam have prime spots near the front; Chloe,
crocheting in a chair, watches with intent calm; Meg and
Michael are together on a couch in the second row.

                         SAM
                      (outraged)
          What! What was that? What are they
          calling that?

                         CHLOE
          Clipping.

                         HAROLD
          That was a clean hit!

                         CHLOE
                      (shakes her head)
          He clipped him.

                         SAM
                      (to Chloe)
          What the fuck are you talking --
                      (catches himself)
          I'm sorry, Chloe.

She waves it off. The Referee, on TV, confirms it: Clipping.
Chloe smiles down at her crocheting.

                         HAROLD
          Where the hell is Nick? I can't
          believe he's missing this.

                         MICHAEL
                      (to TV)
          Come on, Blue, you're not supposed
          to fold 'till the fourth quarter.

118   EXT. SECOND FLOOR VERANDAH - DAY   118

Sarah and Karen sit in a corner of the verandah, talking.

                         SARAH
          I sometimes wonder if maybe I was just
          sick of being such a good girl. I can
          always be counted on to do the right
          thing. That's a disgusting curse. I
                      (MORE)

probably thought that Alex could touch
that part of me that was unpredictable.
And magic. The part I was always afraid
of. Who knows if it's even there.
                    (she folds her legs under her)
When it was over, everything went back
the way it was before. That's what we
all said, that's what we agreed upon.
I was sorry that everybody had to know
about it. That was as much my fault
as anything. But, of course, things
weren't really the same. Alex withdrew
from me then. I was probably different
with him. We never wanted Harold to
think ... well, you can imagine. So
we had finally consummated --
                    (makes a face)
-- this ancient, lurking passion. And
all it had done was put up a wall in
our friendship.

119 INT. DEN - DAY   119

The game and the watchers have calmed down a little. On-screen,
Michigan attempts a rare pass and is intercepted. Harold lets
the popcorn dribble from his hand in disgust. Meg sinks back
into the couch. Michael slides down a little too, so they have
a tiny modicum of privacy and gives her an odd look. She's
quizzical.

                    MEG
          What? I didn't throw the ball.

                    MICHAEL
                    (hushed tone)
          So, what am I, chopped liver?

                    MEG
                    (mystified)
          What are you talking about?

                    MICHAEL
          You know.

                    MEG
          No, I don't.

                    MICHAEL
          You know --

He makes a cradling gesture with his arms and begins rocking
their invisible child. Meg can't believe what she's seeing.
Her head lolls away in stupefaction. Her tone is hushed.

                    MEG
                    (drawn out)
          Michael!

                         MICHAEL
          You asked Sam.

                         MEG
                      (mortified)
          What, is it published somewhere?
          On the nightly news?

                         MICHAEL
          Look, you know we can do it. We've
          done it.

Meg rolls her eyes, he misunderstands.

                         MICHAEL
          You remember? The March on Washington?
                      (tickles her, slyly)
          The Armies of the Night?

She bats his hands away.

                         MEG
          I remember.

                         MICHAEL
          I thought you'd be grateful.

                         MEG
          You're sweeping me off my feet.

                         MICHAEL
                      (a little too loud)
          I thought you wanted a kid.

Sam is reaching for a ball flipped to him by Harold; it goes
through his hands, incomplete. Chloe politely watches the game.

                         MEG
          Michael, I thank you.
                      (puts a hand on his leg)
          This is a big decision. Let me get
          back to you in the third quarter.

She gets up and leaves.

120 EXT. FRONT LAWN (THE SUMMER HOUSE) - DAY   120

Halftime. Harold, Michael and Sam are tossing the football
around with unreasonable spectator vigor. Meg comes out and
stands on the verandah watching. Michael notices her and poses
playfully, showing off the muscles he could hand down to their
progeny. She waves him off, laughing, then notices something
up the block which distresses her greatly.

WHAT SHE SEES: Nick's Porsche is pulling slowly up to the
curb, followed closely by a police car.

                              MEG (O.S.)
          Oh-oh.

Meg comes off the porch and moves toward them as Nick and the
young cop, PETER, get out of their cars. The men notice now,
too, and come up to the cars. Peter speaks with a southern
drawl which he is exaggerating for the occasion. Harold's
natural accent deepens for this conversation. Nick is hostile,
belligerent.

                              HAROLD
          Hi, Peter.

                              PETER
          How're you doing, Harold. This fella
          claims to be one of your guests. That
          true?

                              HAROLD
          That depends. What'd he do?

                              PETER
          For one thing, he ran a red light.

                              NICK
          No I didn't.

                              PETER
          Then he became abusive to me,
          verbally.

                              NICK
          What, you got etiquette laws down
          here? Twenty-five bucks he's hitting
          me for.

                              PETER
          But the main thing is he looks like
          he could be one of them Yankee drug
          dealers we sometimes get passing
          through on their way to Florida.

                              NICK
                    (indicating Meg)
          Here's my attorney. I don't have to
          take that slanderous talk.

                              MEG
                    (professional voice)
          Uh ... excuse me officer, that's true.
          Do you have, uh, probable cause for, uh, --

Peter is looking beyond her at Sam.

                              PETER
          You J. T. Lancer?

                         SAM
          Yes sir, officer.

                         PETER
                      (to Meg)
          What's that make you -- Perry Mason?

                         HAROLD
          He looks a little suspicious to me,
          too. What do you say we take him
          out back and beat the shit out of
          him? But we gotta hurry. The second
          half of the Michigan game is about to
          start.

                         PETER
          Yeah? Who's winning?

                         HAROLD
          Michigan, temporarily.

                         PETER
          That'll change. How's Sarah?

                         HAROLD
          Okay.

                         PETER
          Real sorry to hear about Alex.

                         HAROLD
          Thanks, Peter.

                         PETER
          You know, I'd be willing to let this
          whole thing drop, if you could persuade
          Mr. Lancer here to show me how he hops
          into that sportscar of his on TV.

Sam laughs it off.

                         PETER
          I'd really appreciate it. I see that
          every week and I've always wondered.
          Myself, I always have to open up the
          door.

Harold is laughing now, with Michael.

                         NICK
          Don't do it, Sam.

                         SAM
                      (admonishing)
          Nick.

Sarah has come to the window. We are looking down on the scene
at the curb over her shoulder. The crowd around Nick's car
opens up. Nick grudgingly gets out of the way. Sam steps
back and sets himself uncertainly.

                    SARAH
          I don't believe this.

Sam runs up and hops toward the car. His left leg catches on
the door and he sprawls into the car, smashing his right arm
against the door. He lays there limply as the group crowds
around. Sarah has flinched on impact.

                    SARAH
          I knew it.

She goes to the closet, snatches up a black doctor's bag, and
heads down.

122 EXT. FRONT LAWN - DAY   122

Michael and Meg help Sam, his right arm bleeding, toward the
house. Sarah comes out on the verandah and holds the front
door open for them. Peter is back in his car and Harold is
speaking to him through the window.

                    PETER
               (accent lighter)
          Sorry about that. I thought they could
          really do that stuff.

                    HAROLD
          It's not your fault.

Peter drives off and Harold turns back toward the house. Nick
is wiping up some blood from the front seat of the Porsche.

                    NICK
          Since when did you get so friendly
          with cops?

Harold stops on his way toward the house. He looks at Nick with
barely controlled fury and disgust. He doesn't want to explode.
He starts away again.

                    NICK
               (reading it)
          What?

                    HAROLD
               (whirls on him)
          You know you're fucking stupid! First
          of all, that cop has twice kept this
          house from being ripped off. He happens
          to be an incredible guy. And you --

                                            CONTINUED:

He looks toward the house, pained. He doesn't want to go on.   122
He starts walking briskly toward the steps. Nick follows him
aggressively.

                    NICK
                (challenging)
         Come on, Harold, what is it?

Harold stops on the porch steps and looks down at Nick. He
controls the volume of his voice, so as not to share it with
those inside, but he is furious.

                    HAROLD
         What is it with you? Is jail another
         experience you want to try -- see
         what that's like?

He shakes his head, starts to go inside, stops and turns back
to Nick.

                    HAROLD
         You know, I live here. This place
         means something to me. I'm dug in.
         I don't need this shit.

Harold goes inside, slamming the door. Nick just stands there.

123 INT. KITCHEN - DAY   123

Meg watches as Sarah finishes expertly cleaning and bandaging
the nasty cut on Sam's arm. Sarah's hands are wonderfully
dexterous and confident. Meg and Sam appreciate that with a
kind of glee, proud of her skills. The ROAR of the game comes
from the other room.

                    SAM
         You know I really can do it. It's
         these damn running shoes that are
         so good for you. Practically
         killed me.

                    SARAH
                (mock solicitous)
         We know you can, Sammy.

                    MEG
                (laughs)
         Being a private eye is dangerous work.

There is a crazed CHEER from the den. Sam is antsy.

                    SAM
                (to Sarah)
         I gotta get back in the game, coach.

                                                    CONTINUED:

She releases him with an "all done" gesture. He pops up and   123
heads for the den.

                         SARAH
              Walk!

He throws her a look and goes into the den, passing Michael
who just sticks his head into the kitchen.

                         MICHAEL
                    (to Meg)
              You know, we're deep in the third
              quarter.

Meg reacts with a face.

                         MICHAEL
                    (backing out)
              Just testing you! A little joke.

He is gone and the women are alone. Sarah cleans up her
supplies.

                         MEG
              Michael has graciously agreed to act
              as stud for me. A repeat performance.

Sarah is stopped by this news.

                         SARAH
              He didn't say that, did he?

                         MEG
              It was almost that romantic.

                         SARAH
                    (grimaces)
              So whatcha gonna do?

Meg is silent for several moments. She looks at Sarah, her
mind working.

                         MEG
              Nah ... I can't do it with Michael.
              Too much history there. It's not
              right.
                    (Sarah nods)
              I can't believe this, I'm deciding
              this this second, as we speak.

Sarah puts her arm around her.

                         MEG
              It's not going to happen this week-
              end. Maybe this is a sign from God
              that I should reconsider.
                    (a beat)
                         (MORE)

MEG (CONT'D)
Too bad I'm an atheist.

Sarah hugs her.

125 INT. LIVING ROOM - DAY   125

Chloe is doing the same tortuous dancer's stretches as when we
first saw her in the main title, and in exactly the same place
on the rug. But now, Nick is VIDEOTAPING her and we see part
of this scene on the CAMERA MONITOR and part in the room. Chloe
is sweating and her speech is broken by her exertion.

CHLOE
Like what?

CONTINUED:

                              NICK   125
                    Anything -- just say anything. Tell
                    us about your past.

                              CHLOE
                    I used to live with Alex.

                              NICK
                    Before that.

                              CHLOE
                    Before that? Randy.
                              (pauses, stretches)
                    I don't like talking about my past
                    as much as you guys do.·

                              NICK
                    Okay, I'll buy that. Can you tell
                    us anything about Alex?

                              CHLOE
                    Well, he was cute ... He said we
                    made a good couple because I had
                    no expectations, and he had too
                    many.

126 INT. DEN - DAY   126

     TV SCREEN. Chloe's interview continues as the tape of it plays.

                              CHLOE (ON TAPE)
                    He believed in reincarnation.

                              NICK (ON TAPE)
                    Yeah?

                              CHLOE (ON TAPE)
                    He never ate meat. He said he was
                    afraid he was going to come back as
                    a steak.

     The unseen watchers in the den laugh at this.

                              NICK (ON TAPE)
                    What else?

                              CHLOE (ON TAPE)
                    He said maybe he should have accepted
                    the Rutledge Fellowship.

     On the tape and in the room, there are several silent moments.
     On the tape, Chloe pauses in her stretching and peers at Nick,
     unseen behind the camera.

                                                            CONTINUED:

                          CHLOE (ON TAPE)
                            (gently)
                   What's the matter, Nick?

The tape ends abruptly, replaced by static snow. Now, for the
first time, we see the watchers in the den: Sarah, Nick, Harold
and Michael. They are very quiet.

127   EXT. DRIVEWAY - EVENING   127

Sam is waiting out by the jeep, moving around restlessly, all
alone. Now something occurs to him: he looks around, determines
he's alone, then takes a tentative, measuring run - up to the
open driver's door of the jeep, as though practicing for some
future leap into it, Lancer-style. Karen comes out of the house
and Sam abruptly stops, embarrassed. As she approaches in the
half-light, he is awestruck -- she looks especially pretty
right now, her newly-done hair meticulously casual, very flat-
tering. She walks up very close to him and he can not resist
taking her in his arms, Lancer-style; this maneuver he does
very well indeed.

                          SAM
                   The biggest mistake I ever made in
                   my life was not trying harder to
                   steal you away from Nick.

                          KAREN
                   You know, I always wanted you to try.

                          SAM
                            (surprised)
                   No ... I never had that feeling.

                          KAREN
                   I guess you weren't paying attention.

This is rather big news to Sam. He looks at her thoughtfully.

                          SAM
                   Well, it's a little late now.

                          KAREN
                   Is it?

Now Sam is really thrown. He involuntarily lets her go and
peers, questioningly, into her eyes.

                          SAM
                   What are you saying?

                          KAREN
                   I think you know. I think you've
                   known this whole weekend.

                                                        CONTINUED:

His mind races, trying to figure out what exactly he's known.   127

                    SAM
          You mean, you and Richard ...?

She nods.

                    KAREN
          You see? You've always been able
          to read me. You know my life with
          Richard isn't working.

                    SAM
               (nonplussed)
          ... I could tell you weren't com-
          pletely ... but, I didn't think ...

                    KAREN
               (very quietly)
          I'm going to leave him.

Sam looks faint. Harold comes bouncing out of the house toward
them in high spirits.

                    HAROLD
          Okay, Sam, let's get the Wonton Express
          rolling here. Karen, you wanna take a
          ride?

Sam, still stunned, looks in confusion between Harold and Karen.
He doesn't know if he should take off right now. Karen speaks
to Harold but looks only at Sam. There is a romantic lilt in
her voice.

                    KAREN
          No, you go ahead ... I'll be right
          here.

She steps slowly away from Sam. Sam, in a daze, goes around to
the passenger door.

                    HAROLD
               (to Sam)
          Just climb in there regular, okay,
          Sam?

They get in and Harold pulls out, slamming a ROCK 'N ROLL cassette
into the dash.

128   EXT. BEACHFRONT ROAD - EVENING   128

The jeep tools along the beachfront to the beat of the music.

129   INT. JEEP - EVENING   129

Harold rocks in his seat to the MUSIC. Sam still looks bamboozled.

                                              CONTINUED:

CONTINUED: -86-

                              HAROLD   129
                        (indicates tape deck)
                  Listen to that stuff. Remember when
                  we saw them at Cobo? You probably
                  don't, you were hallucinating pretty
                  heavy that night.
                        (no response from Sam)
                  And we didn't even have any drugs.
                  Ba-boom!

He delivers this last line like a stand-up comic. Sam seems not
to have heard any of this.

                              SAM
                  Have you noticed anything unusual
                  about this weekend?

                              HAROLD
                  You mean other than Alex dying and all?

                              SAM
                  I've been getting some pretty weird
                  propositions around here.

                              HAROLD
                  Yeah?

                              SAM
                  I don't think I could live down here
                  all the time.

130 OMITTED   130*

131 OMITTED   131*

132   EXT.   THE SUMMER HOUSE (DINING ROOM WINDOWS) - NIGHT   -87-   132

Starting at a distance; we MOVE SLOWLY IN on the golden glow
emanating from the dining room. The group is in there, the
refuse of their Chinese meal heaped about the table. Lots of
empty wine bottles and beer cans as partial explanation of the
raucous good cheer we see in pantomime. When we get CLOSE TO
THE WINDOWS, we see that they are taking turns opening their
fortune cookies and reading their fortunes to the group. As
the CAMERA REACHES THE WINDOW, Michael is cracking his cookie
and the others are focusing on him, though the relentless
comments never really abate.

133   INT. DINING ROOM   133

Michael motions for relative quiet and reads his fortune.

                    MICHAEL
                   (reading)
          "Friendship is the bread of life ..."

"Ooohs" and "Aaahs" for the sappy message; a "How true!" and
a "I thought beer was the bread of friendship or something".
Michael motions for quiet; he's not done --

                    MICHAEL
                   (reading)
          "... but money is the honey."

                    SARAH
                  (through the laughter)
          It doesn't say that!

Michael offers it to her as proof; in fact, it does say that.

                    SARAH
          Jesus! Even the fortune cookie people
          have gone cynical.

                    HAROLD
          That's not cynical, it's pragmatic.

                    MICHAEL
          I think it's touching.

134   EXT. GARBAGE CANS - BACKYARD/GARAGE - NIGHT   134

Karen and Sam carry the dinner refuse across the lawn. They
look oddly romantic in the moonlight, this pretty couple, each
with an armload of garbage. Silently, they deposit their bags
in the cans. When their hands are free again, they look at

CONTINUED:

each other a moment across the lids. Then Sam grabs Karen   134
strongly in his arms and turns her into the shadows of the
garage, pressing her against the wall and kissing her passionately.
Finally, the kiss breaks --

                    SAM
                (husky voiced)
        There's nothing I'd rather do right
        now than make love to you ...
                (kisses her forehead)
        ... and, when we were done, take
        you into my life. Have you and your
        boys come out to L.A. and move into
        my house. There's plenty of room
        there. It's lovely.

He holds her close to him.

                    SAM
        ... But I can't do that.

She holds him at arms length and looks at him questioningly.

                    SAM
        It has to do with Robin.

Again, she queries him silently.

                    SAM
        No, it's not that. My marriage is
        completely kaput!
                (gathers himself for a speech)
        When Robin and I broke up, I had a
        million good reasons, a million little
        things that were wrong with her,
        wrong with us ...
                (a beat for effect)
        ... But when I think about it now,
        when I see my daughter now with her
        new father ... I realize that what
        broke us up, what really did it --
        and this is hard for me to admit
        to myself even now -- what did it
        was ... boredom. I couldn't stick
        with it. I'd hate to see you make
        the same mistake.

She looks at him, noncommittal.

                    SAM
        You're a better person than that.

                    KAREN
        Don't give me that shit.

He reacts as if slapped. She looks around, her indignation   134
growing. She just can't hold her tongue.

                    KAREN
          For fifteen years you've been <u>acting</u>
          like I'm the one you really wanted,
          and you've made sure that everybody
          knows it. Now, I come down here --

She breaks off, perhaps because she realizes what she's about
to say. She gives him a look and walks away toward the house.
He does not follow.

135   INT. KITCHEN - NIGHT   135

Harold, Sarah and Meg are in here cleaning up. Harold is on
the phone with his daughter. Meg and Sarah gleefully follow
that conversation through his responses.

                    HAROLD
          ... Don't be mad at him, Molly. It's
          <u>called</u> an "anus" ... I know it's boring
          to hear twenty times in a row. Just
          ignore him, honey ... Okay ... Yes,
          she's right here. Just a minute.

Harold holds out the receiver, but it is to Meg, not Sarah.
Meg, pleased, takes the phone.

                    MEG
               (into phone)
          Hello muffin ... oh you got it, huh?
               (Meg giggles)
          ... I'm so glad. I saw it and I
          said I have only one friend in the
          world who could really appreciate
          this ... Well, it will be our little
          secret.

Meg continues to talk into the phone, but her words are drowned
out by the opening chords of a ROCK SONG. The MUSIC grows, as
the chat continues. We see Sarah watching her friend talk to
her daughter; she is pleased and touched by the moment. She
looks over at Harold who is unaware of her glance. He too is
enjoying it. Sarah regards him thoughtfully.

136   INT. LIVING ROOM - NIGHT   136

The MUSIC continues as the CAMERA MOVES CLOSELY through the
dirty ashtrays, empty coffee cups, half-filled wine glasses, and
crumpled rolling papers of a long evening's talk. It is MUCH
LATER and the entire group is sprawled about the room in various
stages of relaxation and inebriation. Bright new running shoes
have been shucked in little piles. A large joint is slowly

passed around the room; several people hand it on without a
toke -- they've either had enough or they're favoring alcohol.
Their TALK is a growing murmur underneath the strains of the
MUSIC. Slowly, the volume relationship switches as the MUSIC
recedes and the TALK suddenly becomes very clear, with --

                    NICK
          So what would that have meant?

                    MEG
                 (upset)
          What do you mean? It would have
          told us something.

                    HAROLD
          What are you talking about?

                    NICK
          Meg is pissed off 'cause Alex didn't
          leave us a suicide note.
                 (to Meg)
          You think he could have summed up
          his reasons in a note?

                    MICHAEL
          Maybe a long note.
                 (takes a toke)
          I can sum up people's whole lives in
          thirty-two paragraphs. I once did
          an entire rock band in a page and a
          half. And they had two drummers.

                    SAM
                 (angry, to Michael)
          Why do you think this is funny? One
          of our best friends has decided to
          kill himself and we don't have a
          fucking clue as to why.

                    NICK
          You never know why anyone does any-
          thing. I don't know why I chose these
          socks this morning.

                    SAM
          That's a nice equation -- your socks
          and Alex's death.

                    HAROLD
          They are pretty sad socks.

Sam gives him a look.

                    MICHAEL
          I believe the old theory that every-
          body does everything in order to get
          laid.

                              KAREN
          Who said that -- Freud?

                              MICHAEL
          No, I did.

                              NICK
          I don't do anything to get laid.

                              SAM
          You don't _do_ anything.

                              NICK
          I do something. I spend long hours at
          risky, boring work of a totally inde-
          fensible nature -- so watch it. I
          have my pride.

                              MEG
                    (quietly)
          All I'm saying is, how could we have
          let Alex slip away like that?

                              MICHAEL
          Maybe he let us slip away. I never
          heard from him.

                              SAM
          Did he hear from you?

                              MICHAEL
          I tried plenty. He resisted it.

                              HAROLD
          It's true. We saw him a lot, but he
          didn't tell us much. Not me, anyway.
          I can't speak for Sarah.

                              SARAH
          I knew he was unhappy, but that doesn't
          tell you much. I had no idea how bad
          it was.
                    (her eyes flick over Chloe for
                     only a moment)
          I think he purposely wanted to cut off
          from all of us because he was so unhappy
          with where he was at.

                              KAREN
          Is that true, Chloe? Did you feel that?

                              CHLOE
                    (thinks about it)
          I don't know. We had some good times.
                    (MORE)

CHLOE (CONT'D)
I haven't met that many happy people
in my life. How do they act?

SAM
I'm sitting here and I realize I don't
even know what he was doing with his
time these last five years. I remember
he left that caseworker job in Boston,
but, Christ, that must have been '78
or so. And I don't even know why he
started doing that. The guy was a
scientific genius -- what was he doing
welfare work for? Then what -- con-
struction or something?
          (Harold confirms it)
What was that all about?

SARAH
He didn't know what to do.

MICHAEL
I can relate to that.

MEG
Well, I did talk to him a lot and he
always seemed real happy. He gave me
that definite impression.

MICHAEL
Oh, so now he's a lying son-of-a-bitch?

Harold smiles, despite himself. Meg and Sam are unamused.

NICK
          (to Sam)
What do you think -- if you'd been
in touch with him you could have saved
his life? You have that kind of effect
on the people in your life? Keep them
all jolly, do you? Wise up, turkeys,
we're all alone out there. And tomorrow
we're going out there again. I think
it was damn straight of Alex not to cook
up some neat, phoney, Reader's Digest
condensation of his screwed-up life for
our entertainment. I'm so sick of
people selling their psyches for a little
attention. He was classier than that.

SARAH
Yeah, that was a real classy number he
pulled up in the bathtub.

NICK
Hey, you know for some people it's not
a question of <u>why</u> to kill yourself, but
<u>why</u> <u>not</u>.

CONTINUED:

                          SAM
          Give me a break, Nick. Spare us the
          tragic existential pose.

                          NICK
          Sorry, Sam, didn't mean to get into
          your area.

                          HAROLD
          Now, calm down, boys. We're all
          friends here.

Nick laughs at that.

                          MICHAEL.
          This is a well-known dynamic. Seen it
          a million times. Some people ease the
          pain of separation by denigrating the
          relationship.

                          NICK
                    (withering)
          You're so deep.

Michael just smiles; Nick doesn't bother him.

                          MEG
          I think Michael's right. I feel shitty
          tonight about ten different ways. I
          don't want to let this go.

Sarah puts a hand on Meg.

                          MICHAEL
          That's healthy. The only way to avoid
          pain like that is to pretend you don't
          care. I know. I've left more places
          than you'll ever go to.

                          NICK
                    (to Sam, refers to Michael)
          Give him your "pose" line, Sam. There's
          the existential man for you.
                    (to Michael)
          You're one tough cookie, aren't you? I
          could say you're one cold, manipulative,
          using guy and it wouldn't bother you a
          bit.

                          MICHAEL
                    (smiles)
          I'm deeply hurt.

                          HAROLD
          At least our last night is going to be
          a fun one.

                          SARAH
          Please don't do this, guys.

                          KAREN
                       (peacemaker)
          This is happening because we all really
          miss him and we're really hurting.

                          NICK
          I think that's a crock of shit. I
          think we're afraid just the opposite
          is true. Alex died for most of us a
          long time ago.

                          SAM
                   (angry, defending Karen)
          I think you're a crock of shit. Don't
          speak for me or anybody else. You
          hate your life, that's your problem.
          Don't tell us what we feel.

                          NICK
                       (gleeful)
          That's it! That's all I'm saying --
          "if I hate my life, that's my problem."
          Too bad you weren't around to comfort
          Alex just as compassionately.

Sam stands up, suddenly.

                          SAM
          Nick, we go back a long way and I'm
          not going to piss that away because
          you're higher than a kite.

                          NICK
          Wrong. A long time ago we knew each
          other for a short period. You don't
          know anything about me. It was easy
          to get along back then. No one ever
          had a cushier berth than we did. It's
          not surprising our friendship could·
          survive that. It's only out here in
          the world that it gets tough.

                          HAROLD
          Nick.

                          SAM
                       (to Nick)
          I don't care what you say. I know
          I've loved you and everyone here.
          And I'll believe that 'till I kick.

He walks out of the room and slams out the front door. The   136
others watch, pained.

                    KAREN
                  (to Nick)
          What's wrong with you? What's
          happened to you?

                    NICK
               (points at her, pleased)
          That's all I'm saying. How many
          times are you going to make my point
          for me?

Karen gets up and goes after Sam.

137   EXT. BEACHFRONT - NIGHT   137

Sam walks alone in the moonlight along the beachfront.

                    KAREN (O.S.)
          Sam! Wait.

Sam turns and waits. Karen comes up and stops a few feet from
him. They look at each other. Then Karen slips under his arm
and they walk on, together.

138   INT. LIVING ROOM - NIGHT   138

The tension level here has dropped.

                    MEG
                  (to Nick, quietly)
          Yeah, I guess I do believe you can
          help people. Sorry about that.

Harold nods. He agrees with her.

                    SARAH
                  (getting up)
          I do too, Nick. Not that we can save
          people. Probably not. But we can do
          what we can do. That's how I feel.
          So lay into me now. Really let me have
          it.

                    NICK
          Hey, I was just trying to keep the con-
          versation lively.
                  (Michael smiles, looks at him)
          I know, you are Spartacus too.

                    MICHAEL
          I'm willing to go with the majority. What
          goes around comes around, you know.

CONTINUED:

Sarah is headed for the kitchen.   138

                    NICK
               (calls after her)
          So you're gonna continue to love me
          no matter what, huh?

                    SARAH
               (over her shoulder)
          Just don't cross me. Harold, would
          you give me a hand in here?

She disappears into the kitchen. Harold gets up and follows
her. Meg gets slowly to her feet, woozy.

                    MEG
          I think I've had enough.

139   INT. KITCHEN   139

Sarah is fixing up the coffee machine. She hits bottom in the
large coffee can and goes into the dark pantry. Harold comes
in, looks for her and steps to the door of the pantry. Sarah's
arms come out and pull him in.

140   INT. PANTRY   140

Only the light from the kitchen illuminates their embrace.
Sarah kisses the surprised man.

                    SARAH
          I love you very much.

                    HAROLD
          Hey, I'm yours.

                    SARAH
          Harold, I want you to do something
          for me.

                    HAROLD
          Anything. I'll even marry you if
          you want. Wait. I already did that.

                    SARAH
               (hugs him tight)
          Yes, you did ... thank god.
               (a beat)
          It's about Meg.

The MUSIC begins again -- ROCK 'N ROLL. It continues --

141   INT. LIVING ROOM - NIGHT   141

Michael sits alone in the corner of the room with the video
equipment. He is reading the instruction manual with stoned

                                              CONTINUED:

eyes; he's having comprehension problems. Behind him, Chloe   141
has risen and is now standing before Nick.

AT NICK AND CHLOE, she takes his hand. Nick looks at their hands.

                    NICK
          Where to?

Chloe indicates upstairs.

                    NICK
          You know I don't do anything.

Chloe "shh's" him and draws him out of his chair.

142   INT. MAID'S ROOM - NIGHT   142

Meg is getting undressed. There is a KNOCK at the door.

                    SARAH (O.S.)
          It's me.

                    MEG
          Come on in, no one else will.

Sarah comes in. She stands near the door, smiling.

143   EXT. BEACH - NIGHT   143

Sam and Karen are rolling on the sand, vigorously entwined,
working at their clothes.

144   INT. MASTER BEDROOM - NIGHT   144

Harold sits on the bed in his undershorts, nervous. There is
a TAP on the door and Meg comes in, closing the door behind her.
She is wearing the flannel robe we saw on Thursday night, which
Harold had declared his affection for. Meg models it for him
shyly. Harold remembers his manners and jumps up. He takes
her hand and leads her toward the bed, a little formal.

                    HAROLD
          This bed has been lucky for Sarah
          and me.

                    MEG
          I've got to try to relax.

                    HAROLD
          Yeah. I think I just forgot how
          to do it.

They sit on the bed and look at each other. Meg laughs, just
for a second. Harold wants to know why.

                                                    CONTINUED:

                          MEG   144
          It won't sound like I mean it.
               (he encourages her)
          Well ... I feel like I got a great
          break on a used car.

145 INT. CHLOE'S ROOM - NIGHT   145

Nick and Chloe are standing before the crowded closet. One half
of it contains Chloe's clothes, but their attention is on the
other half -- the well-worn wardrobe of the late Alex Marshall.
Chloe calmly slides the hangers along the pole, systematically
showing Nick each shirt, each pair of jeans. Occasionally, Nick
interrupts her murmured commentary to note an item. They're
just looking. Now Chloe comes to a worn leather jacket. She
turns toward Nick to display it better. He remembers it well.
For the first time, we see tears on Chloe's face.

146 EXT. BEACH - NIGHT   146

Sam and Karen make hot, passionate love on the cold beach.

147 INT. MASTER BEDROOM   147

Meg and Harold make sweet, gentle love on the warm bed.

148 INT. DEN   148

TV SCREEN. We see a tape shot in the living room. Sarah, giddy,
waits on the couch as Michael appears from behind camera and
carefully positions himself next to her, peering back at the
camera.

                  MICHAEL (ON TAPE)
               (toward camera)
      ... This should work ...
               (to Sarah, conversational)
      ... Well, Sarah, here we are ...
               (she nods)
      ... I must tell you, I'm picking up
     vibrations here at the house, and I
     am almost certain there is sex going
     on around here ...
               (she laughs)
      ... Sarah, have I ever told you how
     beautiful your eyes are?

She laughs and pushes him away. He falls momentarily out of
camera range, then pops back up.

                  SARAH (ON TAPE)
      So, Michael, tell me about your club.

                  MICHAEL (ON TAPE)
     Ah, forget it. Fuck the club. I can't
              (MORE)

            MICHAEL (ON TAPE)(CONT'D)
deal with those hours. It'd be nothing
but aggravation. And let's say it becomes really successful, right? I be-
come a star. What happens? <u>People
Magazine</u> will send some nasty schmuck
like me to do an interview. Big fucking
deal. Nah, I'm going back to my novel.
I'm going to write about this weekend.

            SARAH (ON TAPE)
      (laughs)
What was it going to be about before?

            MICHAEL (ON TAPE)
Last weekend.

149 DISSOLVE TO: EXT. BEACHFRONT - DAWN (Sunrise over the water) 149

A TITLE APPEARS: <u>SUNDAY</u>

We begin PULLING BACK, to take in the beachfront. We see the
path along the beachfront from a high angle, and then Harold
runs into frame, off on his morning run, and we continue
PULLING BACK into --

150 INT. MASTER BEDROOM - MORNING - DAY   150

Sarah, dressed as she was the night before, is standing at the
window, looking out. She watches her husband run away. She
looks over toward the bed.

Meg is sitting there under the covers. She looks at Sarah,
smiling. They're both happy. The room -- in fact, the whole
house -- is bathed in a warm, rosy light this morning.

151 INT. CHLOE'S ROOM - DAY   151

Chloe is asleep in the bed. Nick sits at the desk, slowly going
through a stack of Alex's papers and memorabilia. Now he picks
up a yellowed clipping from <u>THE MICHIGAN DAILY</u> newspaper. He
holds it delicately in his fingers and begins to read.

152 INT. DAUGHTER'S BEDROOM (KAREN'S ROOM) - DAY   152

Karen is packing her massive wardrobe neatly into her big suitcase. Sam finishes dressing on the bed. He puts on a shoe.

            KAREN
Maybe if Richard and I bring the boys
out to L.A., you could get us in to
see one of the studios.

            SAM
      (looks at her back a moment)
Yeah, sure. Absolutely. No problem.

CONTINUED:

                              KAREN   152
                  Good ... Richard would like that.

153   INT. HALLWAY - FIRST FLOOR   153

      Michael comes out of the office, newly-awakened and a little
      rocky. He comes down the hall and stops at the entrance to the
      den. He looks out toward the front porch.

154   EXT. PORCH - MICHAEL'S POV - DAY   154

      WHAT HE SEES: Harold, back from his run and soaked with
      sweat, stands out on the porch with Nick. They talk. Harold
      puts a hand on Nick's shoulder and smiles.

      Michael turns and walks into the kitchen.

155   INT. KITCHEN - DAY   155

      Lots of people here: Karen, Meg and Sam are at the table with
      coffee, food and cigarettes. Sarah works at the stove. Michael
      heads for the coffee machine.

                              MICHAEL
                  Good morning, youngsters.

      They greet him.

                              MICHAEL
                  So, how'd everybody sleep last night?
                  Did anybody sleep last night? I know
                  I did. All alone in my big Castro
                  Convertible. I felt like Fidel himself ...
                  except he's probably not so lonely.
                  Slept like a baby. Even wet the bed.

                              SARAH
                  Drink your coffee, Michael.

      Sam finishes writing his address in Meg's address book and slides
      it across the table to her, open. Meg looks at the book.

                              MEG
                  Good. That's great. You'll be
                  hearing from me whether you like
                  it or not.
                          (she reads the address)
                  2352 Vista de la Viejo Compasino.
                  That's cute.

      Nick and Harold come in.

                              HAROLD
                  Good morning, everyone.

                              NICK
                          (to Michael)
                  Look what I found in Alex's papers.

CONTINUED:

Nick hands the yellowed MICHIGAN DAILY clipping to Michael, who 155
smiles as he recognizes it and begins reading it. Nick
continues around until he is behind Sam; he puts his hands
on Sam's shoulders and rubs them in a contrite, conciliatory
gesture. Sam hesitates only a moment before accepting, touching
Nick's hand.

Harold bounces cheerily up to Sarah at the stove and kisses
her on the cheek.

                    HAROLD
          How're you doing, baby?

                    SARAH
              (sotto voce, kidding)
          You don't have to be in such a good
          mood.

Harold laughs. Still sweaty, he moves on to the sink and begins
running the cold water.

                    MEG
              (to Karen)
          I know I'm going to be in Detroit
          on this deal sometime. I'm dying
          to meet your boys.

                    KAREN
          I'd love it.

                    MICHAEL
          You're all welcome in New York City.
          Not in my apartment, you understand,
          but in the city. And I will accompany
          you anywhere. I'll even get you into
          Elaine's.

                    SAM
          I thought Elaine's was dead.

                    MICHAEL
          That's why I can get you guys in.

Nick has taken his coffee to the table.

                    SAM
              (to Michael, indicating clipping)
          What's that?

                    MICHAEL
          This is the column I wrote in the DAILY
          about Alex when he turned down the Rutledge
          Fellowship. You remember it?
              (eyeing clipping)
                    (MORE)

                    MICHAEL (CONT'D)
            This is not bad. Good clean style.
            Lean. Economical. Just the right
            touch of ideological fanaticism.

                    SARAH
            I remember Alex was really angry
            about that.

                    MICHAEL
            What are you talking about? I made
            him famous. You think he saved it
            for twelve years because he hated it?

                    NICK
            He also saved his induction notice.

Sarah moves with a dirty pan to the sink. Harold is there
drinking his water. She turns off the cold, turns on the
hot and begins scouring.

                    MEG
            I'm collecting addresses, Nick. Do
            you have one or should I just take
            down your license plate?

                    NICK
            Well, actually ...

Harold jumps in here. He addresses the room, but he is looking
at Sarah.

                    HAROLD
            You can reach Nick here for a while.
            Nick and Chloe are going to stay here
            and do some work out at the old house.

There is a pregnant silence in the room. Sarah registers Harold's
words, thinks about it a second, and then accepts it with a smile.
Nick has been watching her reaction. She reassures him with a
look. Finally --

                    KAREN
            Well, I guess there's a certain
            symmetry to that.

Nick laughs.

                    HAROLD
            So, what's the flight schedule here?
            Any way to coordinate some of this
            airport transport?

                         NICK
          I'll be glad to drive someone.

                         MEG
          That's fine ... if we can take Harold's
          car ...

                         NICK
          Sure.

                         MEG
          And get Harold to drive it.

                         NICK
          Ahhh...

                         MICHAEL
          That won't be necessary. You see,
          Sarah ... Harold, we took a secret
          vote. We're not leaving, we're never
          leaving.

The group in the kitchen laugh. Harold reacts with mock
horror. Sarah works at the sink. They are together for
one last moment.

                    END TITLE rolls.